THE BO

SE

How to

T C

C

CHICAGO

Library of Congress Cataloging-in-Publication Data

Cowan, Thomas Dale.
    The book of seance : how to reach out to the next
world / Tom Cowan.
        p.   cm.
    ISBN 0-8092-3733-4 (pbk).
    1. Spiritualism.   2. Mediums.   I. Title.
BF1272.C76   1994
133.9'1—dc20   93-46338
                                                    CIP

This book is dedicated to Susan Lee Cohen.

CONTENTS

INTRODUCTION TO
THE SEANCE

THE LIGHTS ARE TURNED OUT, and a single candle, set in the middle of the table, lights the room. Seven people sit around the table, their hands resting lightly on its surface. The February wind blows up from somewhere outside and rattles a loose window. A young woman in her early twenties, seated at the end of the table, sneezes, and her breath flickers the candle flame, casting long, jerky shadows against the walls of the room, making it look as if the bodies of those at the table are bouncing up and down on their chairs—or are there "others" in the room, casting shadows on the wall as they dance in a circle around those seated at the table? The medium, a tall, thin man in his middle fifties, his eyes closed, slumps deeper into his chair, but no one seems to notice except the leader. "He's under," she announces to the others.

In the next few minutes the people in this room will discover whether the evening's gathering will be successful, whether they will contact the recently departed spirit of a man who was killed in an automobile accident a month ago. The man is the brother of a woman at the table. Two of the other people present are friends of the deceased man. The remaining three and the medium, now in trance, are regular members of the group. Twice a month they meet to talk with the dead.

SEANCES LONG AGO

In one form or another the seance has been around a long time, providing a setting in which men and women establish contact with the spirits of the dead and receive messages and information from those who have passed on into the next life. Since the earliest days of human history, people have instinctively created methods for reaching out to the invisible realms to communicate with the spiritual entities who inhabit the greater universe of which our planet is but one little corner.

The Oracle at Delphi in Greece, for example, advised rulers and common people alike, dispensing otherworldly wisdom that she received directly from the spirits. The ancient Celts preserved human skulls through which the spirits of the dead talked about the wonders of the otherworld. In Siberia, tribal people consult the skulls of deceased shamans before making important decisions. In the Old Testament, King Saul visited a famous medium at Endor and witnessed a materialization of the prophet Samuel. Throughout history, men and women have sought out hermits, witches, Gypsies, and fortune-tellers—people who live on the edge of the mainstream culture—for information about loved ones who have passed on to the other side or about their own destinies both here and hereafter.

But you do not need to travel back in time to consult ancient oracles or trek off to remote regions of the earth to find tribal shamans who make contact with the spirit

world. Since the mid-nineteenth century the modern seance has become a popular and effective means of contacting the spirit world right in your living room.

THE MODERN SEANCE

The modern seance looks like any gathering of average
men and women who come together for an evening of
spiritual or visionary work, such as meditation, dream
sharing, guided visualization, or psychic healing. The word
seance comes from the French meaning "to sit," and most
seances are just that: folks sitting around, holding a meeting. People who attend seances, called *sitters*, are like
everyone else: rich and poor, educated and uneducated,
wise and foolish, healthy and ill, intensely committed and
just plain curious. The sitters at a seance run the gamut of
personalities and lifestyles.

In the early days of the seance movement, some of the
most distinguished members of the professional communities attended seances and belonged to spiritualist organizations. Prominent Americans who were interested in seances
and spiritualism included the New York editor Horace
Greeley, writers William Cullen Bryant and James Feni-
more Cooper, Lieut. Governor James Talmadge of New
York, the abolitionist William Lloyd Garrison, and Abra-
ham Lincoln, who held seances in the White House (his
medium and her spirit guides are said to have encouraged
Lincoln to free the slaves). In Europe, spiritualism found
supporters among the socialist reformer Robert Owen;
writers Elizabeth Barrett Browning, Anthony Trollope, and
Arthur Conan Doyle; biologist Alfred Russel Wallace;
literary critic John Ruskin; statesman William Gladstone;
and scientists William Barrett, William Crookes, Oliver
Lodge, and Camille Flammarion. Clearly interest in con-

tacting the dead is not limited to a certain class of individuals or people of certain backgrounds.

The same is true of mediums. They come in all shapes and sizes, ages, sexes, and personal backgrounds. Some cultivate a mysterious aura about them to cater to the popular fantasy that mediums should look like exotic fortune-tellers or romantic Gypsies, while others look like the neighbors you would meet in your local grocery store. You can't tell a good medium from a bad one, the professionals from the amateurs, the quacks from the real McCoys by the way they dress, talk, or act. You can identify the effective mediums only by their success in the seance.

One of the most successful and impressive mediums of all time was Daniel D. Home (pronounced Hume), who was born in Scotland in 1833. When Home was a mere boy of thirteen, he had a vision of Edwin, a close friend, who appeared mysteriously at the foot of his bed. Edwin floated off the floor and made three circles in the air. Although Home had no knowledge about the friend's condition, he had an uncanny intuition that Edwin had died three days earlier and was now appearing to him as a discarnate spirit. He was correct. The boy had died three days earlier.

Four years later, when Home's mother died, tables and chairs began moving around, and mysterious rapping noises were heard in the home where he was living with his aunt and uncle. From then on, Home's reputation as a medium and psychic was well established, and his fame spread throughout Europe and America. Famous literary and political figures knew and admired Home, including the American writers William Cullen Bryant and Nathaniel Hawthorne, the English writers Elizabeth Barrett Browning and Arthur Conan Doyle, the sculptor Hiram

Powers, Napoléon III and the Empress Eugénie, Czar Alexander II, the king of Bavaria, and Pope Pius IX.

Over the course of his life thousands of people witnessed Home's psychic abilities: furniture moved, tables danced around the room, grand pianos floated in the air, chandeliers rattled, musical instruments played by themselves, water splashed out of nowhere, birdsong was heard indoors where there were no birds, and spirit hands appeared and shook hands with the guests or carried objects around the room. How did Home do these things? Home claimed there was no secret to the psychic disturbances and spirit apparitions that occurred around him; strange phenomena just happened when he relaxed and got in the mood. Often he would tell guests they could go on talking and chattering since he didn't seem to need any particular atmosphere to do his work. When he was in trance, and if the conditions were favorable, he could levitate to the ceiling or handle fire without being burned. Often spirits spoke through him to those in the room, answering their most personal, intimate questions, often saying, "Good night, and God bless you," when they departed. Home was a highly accurate and successful medium.

Since the middle of the nineteenth century, seances of one form or another have fascinated people from all walks of life. It doesn't seem to matter whether we believe in them. Even skeptics and detractors cannot resist a popular and successful medium, although they come with different motives and expectations than the believers. Much to their surprise, skeptics have even been known to channel spirits at seances, somewhat unwillingly of course. That is, spirits have sometimes singled out the skeptic at a sitting as the individual through whom they convey messages and information.

The modern seance movement began in 1848 in Hydesville, New York, when the Fox sisters, Catherine and Margaret, convinced a spirit who was haunting their house to answer their questions by rapping according to a certain code. The spirit complied, and they discovered that it was a man who had been murdered there. Soon "spirit rapping" swept the country. The Fox sisters made a successful career out of it. In fact it became a fad and eventually caught on in Europe. Like psychic occurrences before and after them, some of the activities spawned by the Fox sisters were fraudulent and some were genuine.

By the late nineteenth century there was so much interest in psychic phenomena that the Society for Psychical Research was founded in London in 1882. Soon there were similar organizations in America and other countries. In time hundreds of organizations, whose members called themselves *spiritualists*, were founded, some as social clubs, others as officially recognized churches. Spiritualist camps such as the communities at Lily Dale, New York; Ephrata, Pennsylvania; Camp Chesterfield, Indiana; and Camp Cassadega, Florida, were established in rural areas, and these became centers for classes, workshops, and gatherings of professional mediums and laypeople. The camps catered to permanent residents as well as visitors who attended for specific events.

In time the term *spiritualist* took on a religious meaning: a person who subscribed to the belief that departed souls can communicate with the living, usually through a medium. (The term had formerly referred to people who argued that reality was not solely material but had a spiritual component or even a spiritual origin. Philosophers such as Plato, Aristotle, Gottfried Wilhelm Leibniz, Josiah Royce, and Henri Bergson, to mention a few, were exponents of the spiritualist or idealist view.) By the end of the nineteenth century, *spiritualist* meant more than a person who believed in the invisible, nonmaterial aspects of existence; now it was the name given to those who believed the human soul survives death and can continue to participate in the lives of the living. This idea would become, for many people, the basis for religious beliefs and practices.

By the twentieth century, scientists, serious students, and both lay and professional investigators were going to seances and recording their findings in official journals. The results were what we might expect: some seances were hoaxes, others were the genuine article, and some were mixtures of crass showmanship and real spirit contact. Clearly some genuine mediums, with real success at contacting the dead, feel the need to use trickery to enhance their reputation or to ensure a successful seance when they have some reason to suspect that things might not go right. But, oddly enough, resorting to trickery now and then does not seem to discourage spirits from using a medium!

Widespread interest in seances, along with tarot cards and Ouija boards, peaked in the early part of the twentieth century, indicating that, even in the modern world, average men and women continued to be fascinated by the ability to communicate with the dead and to divine information through nonordinary channels. Mediums, spirits, and seances became part of popular culture, from Madam Arcati, the zany medium in Noël Coward's 1941 comedy *Blithe Spirit*, to Whoopi Goldberg's portrayal of the con artist psychic who unwittingly latches on to a real spirit in the 1990 Hollywood movie *Ghost*. Of course the medium, exorcist, and ghostbuster are now stereotypes in Hollywood horror films, instilling unwarranted fear in movie audiences. It is unfortunate that so many people come out of a dark theater into the light of day thinking that the spirits of the dead are malicious, evil creatures who usually look and smell disgusting. Such movies give the spirits of the dead a bad rap, so to speak, since their main purpose is to shock and terrify audiences, not present the truth about seances or the dead.

THE MEDIUM

In every generation some individuals feel drawn to mediumship. These people learn about the next life directly from the spirits themselves and serve as channels for contact and communication between the worlds of the living and the dead. To be a gateway through which the spirits can traverse the boundaries that separate them from us is a noble calling, and in spite of the frauds who discredit the profession, the work of a genuine medium is held in the highest respect by many people. The long history of seances and the intelligent men and women who have taken seances seriously suggest that the subject is worth looking into, if for no other reasons than to assuage our own fears of death and expand our awareness of the marvelous universe in which we live. For many people the medium is a kind of nondenominational minister or facilitator, serving the needs of both the spirit world and the physical world. The medium stands as the link between life here and life beyond.

Over the years many mediums have been studied and tested, many willingly offering themselves for scientific research to advance our knowledge of the paranormal. After decades of study, much remains unknown. Information derived from nonordinary channels, which was once thought to be accessible only through spirits, has now been shown to be part of the normal psychic powers of individuals gifted with strong powers of extrasensory perception. (In other words, it may be "only" E.S.P.) Nevertheless, the fact that some mediums display extraordinary psi capabilities does not rule out the possibility that on some occasions those talents are used to make contact with spirit entities from the invisible realms beyond the grave.

J. B. Rhine, one of the foremost American psi researchers and widely respected for his groundbreaking studies at Duke University, points out that after several generations of research the "question raised by spiritualism must be faced as one of science's greatest problems." On one level the problem concerns the "existence of an accessible spirit world." Put more broadly, says Rhine, it asks us to look into the nature of human existence to see if there is something truly spiritual. And in its most far-reaching implications it is a quest into the very heart of Creation to discover the "presence of anything spiritual or nonphysical in the universe" itself.

But most of this conjecture is moot to anyone who has ever experienced a successful seance. Meeting spirits, most agree, is indeed communicating with a clearly perceived "other." While in the deepest sense it may not matter whether a spirit is another being, a hidden facet of the medium's soul, or extrasensory knowledge, the source of which is another living human, it is important to note that thousands of people who have participated in seances believe, without a doubt, that they have contacted another plane.

GLIMPSES OF THE NEXT WORLD

The doubts and uncertainties of scientists and professional investigators are shared to a lesser degree by some spiritualists themselves. Although there are many whose beliefs in the "accessible spirit world" is unshaken, there are also spiritualists who harbor a certain amount of unbelief, usually because their own encounters with the spirits have not been as dramatic or consistent or convincing as the experiences of others. You need not worry that you have to be "a believer" or witness to a "faith" in spiritualism to take part in seances. Most important, you need not give up your current spiritual beliefs or religious commitments to attend a seance or to develop your mediumistic skills.

People attend seances for all sorts of reasons, but most are looking for reassurance that there is life after death and that human consciousness, or the soul, survives the death of the body. And many people find this reassurance. The old adage that death is a portal through which "no traveler ever returns" is just not true for men and women who have had firsthand experience with spirit communication in seances. When the conditions are right, the spirits come, and the sitters are encouraged and comforted by the heart-felt evidence that life continues after death. No specific religious beliefs are necessary for believing that the spirits of the departed are still in an accessible place beyond the physical earth plane. An open mind and heart, a sense of adventure, and a general suspicion that our ultimate destiny is grander and more interesting than we may have been taught are all you need to bring.

A seance temporarily lifts the "veil between the worlds" so the living and the dead can reunite and speak to one another. It strengthens the perennial hope that life does not end with our last breath and that our spirits do not depart this world forever. Seances confirm the intuitive feeling that our souls are immortal and that death is simply a change of form, an entry into a new and better world.

UNFINISHED BUSINESS

In addition to confirming our beliefs in life after death, seances provide a means for contacting specific spirits, provided the spirits themselves are willing to make such contact. Often people attend seances because they want to reconnect with a recently departed friend or family member to learn if he or she has made a successful transition into the next life. We long for some sign that our loved ones are safe and happy. At times we may be reluctant to let go of those we love, and we expect seances to be a way to hang on to the departed. Such seances are usually not successful, because they don't take into account the wishes of the spirits themselves. Sometimes, recently departed spirits do not want to preserve their links with those they knew in this world. They don't want to hang around as ghosts or apparitions. For them it is time to cut the ties, move on, and begin a new life.

Other spirits, especially those who died suddenly or violently, have unfinished business with people they left behind. For them death came too early, before they completed all they had hoped to achieve in this life. They may still have important things to say to friends or relatives. They may want to ask forgiveness for harm done to others or to explain some behavior that caused trouble for others. They may be curious about what has happened to people they left behind. Some spirits simply want to assure the people they loved that they did truly love them and still love them. Others want to reassure their loved ones that they are all right. For all these reasons spirits may be quite eager to make contact and from what we know of life on the other side, they often need the medium and the group energy of a seance to communicate. It is always important, therefore, to find out the wishes of the spirits and allow them to use the seance for their own needs as well as the needs of the sitters.

A seance is a first step in dealing with hauntings. When contact is made, you can determine whether the strange happenings and eerie feelings connected with a building, garden, crossroads, or grave are being caused by a genuine spirit haunting the place or are the "psychic residue" of a highly charged incident that occurred there years ago. Traumatic or violent events, such as murders and battles, can imprint their energy on an environment, as can bright, joyous occasions, such as celebrations and religious ceremonies. A woodland grove, for example, where our ancestors performed seasonal or monthly rituals at the full moon can still retain that energy. A seance may reveal whether the suspected haunting is a genuine ghost, who it is, and what it needs to be released.

MESSAGES AND HELP FROM BEYOND

Another motive for attending seances is to receive important life messages from the spirit world. Throughout the ages people have looked to mediums, channels, and psychics for advice and instruction on how to live their lives, because these unique individuals have special relationships with spirits guides and otherworldly teachers.

Many spirits are eager to give instructions and teachings, often of a highly ethical and philosophical nature. In recent years this type of information has come through people who prefer the term *channeler* over *medium*, but like mediums, they convey messages from discarnate beings or spirits. A channeler might work privately with single clients or channel in a group that conducts a more or less standard seance.

A medium who has an articulate and perceptive spirit guide can channel teachings of profound importance during a seance, messages about the meaning life or conditions in the next world or what a sitter needs to change to live a more fulfilling and rewarding life. In general we hope that the spirits will use the seance to inform us about what is truly important in life, how we can use this life to advance in wisdom and enlightenment, and what we can do to prepare for the next stage of progress after death.

We need to remember, however, that a person does not suddenly become all-wise and all-knowing by passing into the next world. Death is not a crash course in universal wisdom. After they die, people continue to be pretty much what they were while in this life. If they were well informed and intelligent in this life, they probably will be so in the next life. If they were selfish and self-centered, they may still be. If they were caring and loving people, they are now most likely caring and loving spirits. However, the opportunities for seeing the broader picture and for putting the mundane problems and worries of this life into perspective are far greater for those who are no longer bound up in them. The view from beyond the grave is similar to the view from a mountaintop in that it offers a far more commanding vista.

Our personal problems and worries can look much different from the world of spirits, just as troubles at home tend to subside when we go on vacation or take a brisk walk to get away from them for a while. Death effectively removes the blinders that narrow our vision and understanding in this world. In general the teachings from the spirits, no matter how much or how little those spirits know, can be beneficial and inspiring, provided we keep a balanced, objective attitude and reflect rationally and intelligently on what the spirits tell us.

A seance may be the vehicle for discovering personal spirit guides. If there is someone on the other side who wishes to become your guide or helping spirit, a seance may be his or her opportunity to contact you. We all have helping spirits, who may be the discarnate spirits of people who once lived on earth or spirits that were never incarnate, but we often go through life without ever knowing who our spirit helpers and guardian angels are. In our daily lives we have no forum for meeting them. The seance can be that forum, the primary setting for meeting and communicating with your spirit guides, after which they may spontaneously appear or speak to you outside the seance. The seance is always a safe harbor where you can go for meetings and instructions from those in the otherworld who protect and watch over you.

HEALING POWER

Seances can be used for healing work. Some mediums are natural psychic healers; others rely on the profound healing power of their spirit guides. When a medium functions as a healer, it is usually the spirit operating through the medium that provides the life force or vital energy that a person needs for recovery. The same is true of diagnosis and treatment. It is not the medium but the spirit who evaluates the patient's condition and prescribes the treatment. As with other information from the spirit world, you should treat it as you would any advice from the living. If it seems wrong or inappropriate, you may want to get a second opinion, from either another spirit or a traditional physician.

A healing seance may be conducted for a specific person or used as a general healing ceremony for all the sitters. Attending a healing circle and sharing in the group energy can be very effective, especially for emotional and spiritual problems. The peaceful, calming atmosphere of a healing session revitalizes our spirits, renews our idealism, and motivates us to carry on with the problems of life. When we participate in the blended healing aura of the group, the medium, and the spirits who are present, we feel that we are part of something bigger than ourselves. We get a sense of the mystery of the universe that transcends our own petty worries and troubles.

The spirit world is not far from here. Throughout history, mediums, mystics, psychics, saints, shamans, and other visionaries have caught glimpses of it and reported to others what they found. For the most part they have seen a world of light and beauty, peopled by radiant spirits and the discarnate souls of the once-living who now enjoy bliss and happiness. To attempt to reach that world or communicate with its citizens is a sacred task, not to be undertaken frivolously or for unethical purposes. What we do in this life weaves a web of spiritual connections that will follow us into the next. Our actions create karma; our lives have consequences.

How to Use This Book

Anyone can communicate with the dead. *The Book of Seance* is designed to help you begin your journey on this exciting path. Be aware that some people are better at seance work than others—just as some people are better cooks, artists, or singers than others. Your personality, temperament, health, attitude, energy level, and a myriad of other factors help determine how easily and how well you receive and interpret messages from beyond. You may find that you have a real gift for mediumship. Perhaps you already have a gift and want to become a professional medium. Or you may find that you contribute best to a seance circle as a sitter. Whatever your skill level, you'll find that, as with anything, you get better with practice. Be open to new experiences, and be accepting of what happens to and for you. An experienced, successful medium is not a better person than a new medium.

changed lifestyles." NDE accounts confirm this notion that the soul or spirit leaves the body and passes into another "place" but does not die. The spirit goes on living, but in a different way.

Throughout this book we will honor the fact that the dead are not really *dead*, that they continue to live. However, for practical linguistic purposes, it is necessary to distinguish them from those of us still living in our bodies. The simplest term for referring to them is *the dead*. Although it wraps us in paradox, it is necessary from an earthly point of view to think of them as "those who have died" even though we know they have merely passed over to the other side, into a reality we normally do not perceive except under the right conditions, such as during a seance, in dreams, and in other mystical experiences. Therefore we will refer to them as "dead" even though we know they are still alive.

The second most basic fact about the dead—almost too obvious even to mention—is that their spirits can still communicate with the living. In various ways they are still involved in our lives and to some extent still concerned about the things of earth. Were they not, we would have no encounters with them, either spontaneously or formally, in seances and channeling sessions.

We are told that all spirits have the power to communicate with the living (it is in their nature to do so), but not all make use of this power. Some do not communicate because the Creator does not allow them to, possibly because the Divine Will decrees that, in general, people are meant to live their lives without direct contact with certain spirits. This seems to be a major law of life on the earth plane; namely, we are meant to rely primarily on our own knowledge and skills and those of our mortal companions, with spirit guidance being supplemental or secondary.

Other spirits cannot manifest or communicate with the living because of personal circumstances in their own development. They are given missions, assignments, or experiences for their own evolution or purification, and these activities do not allow them "time" to become involved in our lives. (We will look at the notion of "time" in the spirit world later in this chapter.)

So for various reasons some spirits do not manifest or communicate with us. But from the hundreds of thousands of accounts from people in all walks of life, it is clear that spirits *can* communicate and participate in our lives if they wish to and are allowed to.

Spirits relate that there are various paths leading through the next world, just as many ancient stories suggest. Varieties of spiritual existence await us. Many spirits tell us that the notion that everyone goes to either heaven or hell is too simplistic, denying the rich variety of human experience, both earthly and cosmically. Just as personal lifestyles on earth vary from individual to individual so that no two of us live exactly the same life, so we will discover in the next world destinies that are tailored specifically for our individual needs and desires. We each encounter a unique fate based on the Creator's personal designs for us and on the karmic material that we contribute to it from our lives on earth. Many sacred stories about the afterlife describe these general patterns.

Another familiar account from the spirits is that when we view our lives in their most cosmic sense, we are all evolving toward higher stages of existence. As some put it, we are being purified and perfected through various teachings and experiences both here on earth and in the hereafter so that we will eventually become worthy to approach and merge with the Divine Source. Karma may require that some of those purifying experiences be difficult, per-

these spirits have passed through, but in most cases we can trust their instructions because they are truly messengers sent to assist us. That is, their current mission is to teach us about the mysteries of human life and the greater universe so as to facilitate our own evolution to higher stages of perfection.

In the middle range are spirits who have separated sufficiently from their prior lives to allow them to strive for purification and elevation as their primary goal. "Aspiration after perfection has become the ruling desire," say Kardec's spirit informers about these midlevel beings. While they are in this middle range, spirits may undergo further types of living and learning experiences, in either our universe or some parallel universe. They may, for example, be sent as guardians and guides for the living, to watch over us, inspire us, pull "cosmic strings," so to speak, keeping us on the right path toward our ultimate destiny.

In the bottom rank are what Kardec calls "lower spirits," people recently deceased or not totally resigned to having left their material lives on earth. They are still earth-bound to some degree, still unable to let go of their former loves and passions. Mediums and mystics tell us that what distinguishes unevolved or "young" souls, perhaps in their first incarnation, is their attachment to the things of earth.

Immediately after death, many young souls do not release their former lives sufficiently. They cling to former identities, familiar places, the important people they knew, the projects they were working on and did not complete. For example, a recently deceased man may not want to let go of loved ones, fearing either that the people he loved will not survive alone or, conversely, that he will not be able to walk forward into the next world without the love and support of old friends and family members. People whose lives were filled with anger and hatred may cling to former passions, bitterness, and feuds. The desire to even old scores makes it difficult to move ahead into the spirit world.

Although most spiritual teachings say that the ideal is to "let go completely," there seem to be reasonably well-adjusted spirits on all levels who retain a healthy interest in their former lives. This is particularly true of helping spirits who hang around to protect, guard, or teach people they formerly knew and loved. A young man requested a seance recently because he felt his girlfriend, who had been killed in a car accident, was still around. Her spirit presence worried him because he had heard that people killed unexpectedly can have trouble moving into the next world. At the seance the girlfriend's spirit told the young man that she was not caught between the worlds but that she was hanging around to help him grieve.

Afterward, the medium confirmed that the woman was a "highly evolved soul" and that lingering near her boyfriend was not impeding her evolution in the next life. Not surprisingly, once the man understood what his friend's spirit was doing, he was able to accept the loss and his need to mourn (he had formerly thought it unmanly to show sorrow). After the seance he was able to express his feelings more openly and bring the grieving process to a resolution.

To what degree each spirit must release its former existence may be a personal matter, differing from person to person, and we may not fully understand the differences until we are in the situation ourselves.

Another characteristic of the lower order of spirits is that many of them have an aversion to the next life. Some, in fact, do not even know they are dead. This is particularly true of people who die suddenly or violently. Reports tell us that people unprepared to die may hover in a foggy or semiconscious state for a while and only gradually awaken to their new lives and the realization that, from the point of view of their former lives, they are in fact dead. Some seances perform important work in this respect by helping newly deceased spirits separate from the earth and move through the light into the next world.

A group of sitters on the East Coast has made contact with a particular spirit whom I think of as the Light-Crosser. Like Charon, the Greek ferryman who transported the souls of the dead across the River Styx, the Light-Crosser assists spirits in crossing into the light. The sitters call the Light-Crosser when they are working with a recently deceased soul who needs help. The Light-Crosser always comes, and the medium encourages the troubled soul to look up and find the Light-Crosser and go toward her. The group has had great success working with this spirit and has helped many people release themselves from the earth plane and begin their next life in earnest.

The lower spirits are not "evil" in the sense of being satanic. It would be more accurate to say they can be mischievous, sometimes insulting and jealous of the living, lacking in knowledge, or even able to wish us or do us harm; but they are not the personification of cosmic evil. Allan Kardec explains that the common notion of evil spirits exists because we need allegorical images to understand various phenomena; demons and devils are the allegorical references for the things we find base, disgusting, and loathsome *in ourselves*. We project these traits onto spirits so that we don't have to admit that we are responsible for them. We can even blame devils and demons for the harm that we do.

The spirits told Kardec that the Creator did not create eternally evil spirits who are continually opposed to the goodness of Creation. Instead, all spirits have been created with free will and are placed on the road to perfection, which is acquired through knowledge and experience. Some spirits advance along this road more quickly than others, but all spirits do move forward, each at its own pace. Ignorant and inexperienced spirits on the lower levels may choose to do harm, sow confusion, or behave in disruptive ways, but in so doing they retard their own progress. Even these spirits, Kardec explains, have been created to reach higher levels of perfection and happiness and will do so eventually.

Here is what the spirits who instructed Kardec have to say about the lowest rank of spirits.

> *Some of them are inactive and neutral, not doing either good or evil; others, on the contrary, take pleasure in evil and are delighted when they find an opportunity of doing wrong. Others, again, are frivolous, foolish, fantastic, mischievous rather than wicked, tricksy rather than positively malicious; amusing themselves by mystifying the human beings on whom they are able to act, and causing them various petty annoyances for their own diversion.*

We should keep in mind that the polarities we perceive from our earthly perspective, especially the ones we label "good and evil," may not be diametrically opposed to each other, but play some mutual role in our ultimate evolution. In other words, what we think is bad or evil may, in the long run, be good for us. We will be able to evaluate our experiences and perceptions only when we are further along in our own spiritual development. For now we should simply avoid spirits who do mischief, cause harm, or make life aggravating for us. Later in the book we will learn how to handle annoying, insulting, and trouble-making spirits.

Time and Place

Just as earthly polarities and metaphors have little corre-
spondence with conditions in the next world, so do references to time and space. One of the universally agreed
upon facts about the spirit world, confirmed by spirits and
by mystics who have personally had glimpses into that
world, is that time and space as we know them do not really
exist. Interestingly, physicists who specialize in the world of
subatomic particles have discovered the same thing: even
on earth there are places, infinitesimal and terribly remote
from our ordinary perception, where space-time constructs
simply do not apply. And yet in our dealings with spirits we
have to operate on earth time and in physically determined
places. An obvious case in point is holding a seance. You
have to hold it somewhere and at a certain time. How do
spirits know where we are? How do they know that we are
ready? How do spirits "enter" our space-time world, and
what should we expect of them while they are here?

Again, we have to keep in mind the limitations under
which we are operating and realize that, from our point of
view, spirits have a remarkable degree of freedom that is
denied to us. They can be in more than one place at the
same time; they have access to a wide range of information.
They have their own limitations, of course, some of which
they explain to us, and others we will never comprehend
until we share their experience on the other side. In general, spirits accommodate themselves to our world rather
well. They show up at seances when we are ready, use our
language and concepts, and instruct us in terms that make
sense to us. Nevertheless, there is always the possibility of
misunderstanding on our part, or their part, since we are
coming from two different places, as it were.

Spirits have said that the next life, the world of spirits,
eternity, the kingdom of heaven—call it what you will—is

not so much a place as a state of consciousness. Because it is not geographical or localized, spirits are, in some sense, everywhere at once. They do not have to "come and go," even though that phrase makes the best sense to us in our efforts to describe encounters with them. Even though they are always "here," they are not always manifest. We are unaware of them. When they choose to manifest, it seems as if they have "come."

We might expect that, because spirits are in a state of consciousness rather than in a physical place, they are constantly aware of everything in the universe. But this is not so. In some fashion or other they have to "get" or "tune in to" specific matters. They must "access" information just as we do, and so at any given moment they do not know everything. Even specific memories of their former lives may not be readily available to them, for reasons we will look at in later chapters.

Similarly, time does not exist for spirits as it does for us. They may have some sense of "duration" or the "passing" of events, but we should be wary of equating it with our own experience. They have told us (as have mystics and subatomic physicists) that everything that ever was or will be exists in a timeless present. Both past and future are occurring right now. In fact, there is only the now. It is difficult for us to comprehend this, although people who meditate regularly come close, during meditation and visionary experiences, to participating in the timelessness in which "time" takes place. From our ordinary, daily perspective, however, events occur in a linear fashion, progressing forward from those that have already taken place to those that have not happened yet.

Another important implication of the timeless-placeless nature of the greater universe is that we are all one. As mystics and the great spiritual teachers have taught, my separate existence, my feeling trapped in a specific body and age, is an illusion. Many spiritual and religious traditions try to break this illusion's hold over us by giving us insights into the unity of Creation and the oneness of Creation with the Creator. This is not the place to explore all the ramifications of this great metaphysical truth, except to point out that if we all are one, living in a great web of shared existence, to open the channels of communication between any two beings within the web is not outside the realm of possibility. The links are already there. Theoretically we should be able to communicate with plants, animals, the elements, or anything else just as we communicate with each other. Letting the information flow is the challenge. A seance is one method for creating the conditions in which communication between the living and the dead flows freely and spontaneously.

PREPARING FOR THE MOMENT OF DEATH

Many spiritual traditions warn us that our state of consciousness at the moment of death determines how easily we pass into the next world. Our immediate experiences after death are greatly influenced by our thoughts, attitudes, and the condition of our souls when we die. We find this belief in Asian religions as well as among Christians who pray for a "holy death." Many tribal people hope to use their last breath to sing a personal "death song." In some cultures, as important as the dying person's state of consciousness are the prayers, ceremonies, and practical rituals that the living must perform for someone immediately after death.

Today there is a growing belief that death—where, and how we die—should be, to whatever extent possible, a personal decision. Many people are leaving cold and comfortless hospital units to die at home or in friendlier hospice environments. Some people with terminal illnesses do not want to be kept alive in a comatose state that deprives them of a meaningful departure from their loved ones. Some people are asking to end their own lives legally and safely to assure that they live their last moments in this world and their first moments in the next with dignity.

In many ancient traditions there are "books of the dead," written explicitly to initiate people into the mysteries of the otherworld and prepare them for the moment of death. The Egyptian and Tibetan Books of the Dead, the medieval writings called *ars moriendi,* and the Celtic myths of wonder voyages to the Blessed Isles provide this type of instruction. In tribal societies shamans and spiritual leaders conduct dramatic and often terrifying initiation ceremonies to prepare people, at key points in their lives, for what they can expect when the soul leaves the body.

The modern Western world is unique in being the only major civilization that does not adequately prepare its people for this most important moment in life. In fact we take just the opposite approach. We deny death, shield our young people from it, and try to forget about it until the last possible moment. With cosmetics and surgery we hide the natural processes of aging. We remain oblivious to the deaths of animals and plants that provide our food. And yet, almost perversely, the death industry—providing funeral insurance, wakes, coffins, burial plots, and so forth—is a multimillion-dollar enterprise. What's more, most of our images of death and dying are terribly distorted and misleading, coming from movies, television, and comics that either glamorize and romanticize death or portray it as something horrible beyond belief.

Seances, however, can provide us with a healthy corrective because they allow us to spend time with the spirits

of the recently departed and the higher spirits who are sent
to instruct us about the marvels and wonders that await us
in the next world. Spirit teaching, coupled with accounts
from NDEs, furnish us with vital information about the
hereafter. Rather than being a morose or depressing activity, holding a seance is uplifting, encouraging, and supportive of life's highest values. Many seances are fun and
joyful. Death is only morose or depressing when we are not
prepared to let go and release ourselves from the bonds of
earth, when we fear that nothing in us will survive into the
greater universe that lies beyond the grave.

Of course fear usually springs from not knowing, and
by its very nature death will always harbor an unknown
component. But the wisest teachings throughout the ages
have encouraged us to overcome that fear. In the Middle
Ages, Saint Thomas Aquinas wrote, "Let death be thy
teacher." In the twentieth century Carlos Castaneda's
Yaqui sorcerer, don Juan, tells him that death is "an ally."
The Christian Gospels tell us that death can come either
as a "bridegroom" or as a "thief in the night." It's up to us.
If death can be a powerful ally, teacher, or mate, so can the
spirits who come to us in seances, showing us that death
need not be the thief who robs us of our lives and steals our
loved ones from us.

OUR GREATER COMMUNITY

Human beings cannot live without community. The soli-
tary hermit living an ascetic life is the exception that
proves the rule. We need companionship, love, understanding, help, and challenges from other human beings. Most
of us find community in our families, friends, neighbors,
work associates, and voluntary organizations and clubs, but
these natural associations are not the limits of community.

Currently the definition of *community* is being extended to include "members" that modern people have not traditionally recognized as related to them in any human or intelligent way. We are all part of the ecological community, for example, which includes the natural environment. In this community human beings are but one group among thousands. We lost this understanding somewhere over the last several hundred years. Our ancient ancestors, however, took it for granted that animals, plants, the features of the landscape, the weather, and the seasons were part of the community of all living things. They recognized the intelligent spirit, the living consciousness, in every created thing, even rocks, mountains, water, and fire.

The notion of community as composed of both the living and the dead is also making a comeback. Again we can learn from ancient people who honored the dead, considering them active members of the human community even though they had passed over to the other side. This idea that the human community includes the dead found strong expression in some cultures, giving rise to ancestor worship, personal shrines dedicated to the deceased, sacred days and festivals to honor the dead, and the practice of retaining relics, skulls, or other keepsakes to remember loved ones.

We have not completely lost the belief that the dead are still with us. In most modern countries, there are national holidays to honor the dead. Consider the American Memorial Day, held, significantly, at the height of spring, when our thoughts and feelings turn spontaneously to the renewal of life in nature. In the Catholic tradition the second of November is All Souls' Day. The night before November 1, All Saints' Day, is the Eve of All Hallows, now called Halloween. Originally this was the Celtic New Year, a night when the veil between the worlds of the living and the dead was lifted so that we might communicate with one another more openly. We continue this tradition in a secular way by dressing up as ghosts, skeletons, spooky ghouls and goblins, fairies, witches, and other figures we associate, rightly or wrongly, with the otherworld. A "day of the dead" does not have to be filled with sorrow; it can be a joyful, fun annual reminder that death has no permanent claim over the living.

Many people today are consciously trying to preserve, or create, relationships with the dead. Perhaps because the media have allowed us to see that so many people are dying today—and dying *young* from cancer, AIDS, and cardiovascular problems—there is a renewed concern for not allowing the lives and memories of dear ones to fade. We hold memorial services, maintain graves sites, preserve ashes, keep old photographs of the dead, honor the birthdays and deathdays of loved ones. These are all valuable and worthy practices that serve to preserve or renew our relationships with those who have gone before us.

An area that desperately cries out for a broader definition of community in which we include the dead concerns miscarriages and abortions. Mothers, fathers, and the lost children themselves suffer from not being able to continue the relationship on some spiritual plane, once the possibility for a physical relationship has been ended. In our culture women seldom end a pregnancy in what tribal people call "a sacred manner." In other words, they do not prepare themselves with whatever spiritual practices are meaningful for them: prayer, fasting, meditation, vigil. Nor do they incorporate sacred ritual into their lives after the pregnancy ends to place the event in a sacred context that is broader and deeper than the ordinary life of the parents. Similarly, many parents do not prepare the unborn child for the abortion by talking to it, explaining what will happen and why, and inviting the child's spirit to return perhaps at a better time. Nor are there rituals to honor that child's brief companionship in the parents' lives. A compassionate medium, who understands the difficulties in this type of crisis, can offer immeasurable help.

The spirit of an unborn child is likely to become a lost soul that wanders restlessly between the worlds. Entering the next life in a confused and frightened state, the child may hang around after death, trying to resolve unfinished business. A psychic recently told me about a client who wanted to gather information concerning her stepdaughter, who was still alive. In the session the psychic, whom I will call Rickie, was told by her spirit guide that the stepdaughter had a child who seemed to be going through a very distressful period in her life. Rickie conveyed this information, but the client said that her stepdaughter did not have any children. Rickie's guide insisted there was an unhappy child involved, and then the client remembered that her stepdaughter had had an abortion a few years previously. A seance for the parents and the spirit of the unborn child can be a healing experience for all concerned.

THE SEANCE:
A HARBOR BETWEEN THE WORLDS

Our society needs healthier attitudes toward death, dying, *and the dead.* Seances can help change those attitudes by offering people a chance to reconnect with the spirit of a loved one, either to release it completely from our ordinary lives or to create an ongoing relationship with it that is compatible with both our daily life and the loved one's evolution in the next world.

Seances develop our natural ability to communicate with the spirit world, whether we continue to do so in the formal seance setting or in our own private devotions and rituals. By regularly taking part in seances and practicing the techniques outlined in this book, you can increase your psychic/spiritual awareness, a fundamental quality of human nature and a doorway to communicating with spirits.

A seance creates a supportive environment in which you can explore and understand unexpected encounters with spirits, either in dreams, prayers, or paranormal experiences (such as spontaneous apparitions, which are more common than most people think). In a seance we find a setting for learning more about the ongoing flow of information between the spirit world and our own. Contacts with the dead, whether unexpected or arranged, can become a normal part of our lives, as they should be, because seeing and hearing the spirits of deceased friends and family members is a normal part of the human experience.

Studies conducted with widows and widowers show that nearly half of those interviewed experienced the spontaneous apparition of their deceased partners. Most of these "bereavement contacts," as they are called, occur in the first decade after death, but some take place as many as twenty years later. In 1973 and 1984 the National Opinion Research Center in Chicago conducted interviews of the general public (not people grieving over departed spouses) and discovered that, depending on the population surveyed, anywhere from 25% to 67% had had postmortem contacts with someone deceased. The studies show that the likelihood of having such contact is not related to age, religion, ethnic background, or level of education.

Many people also hear the dead speak to them. In times of trouble or worry we find ourselves spontaneously calling out to a deceased spouse, parent, or other loved one for advice or strength. Each of us in our own way hears an answer. In many cases we find we just "know" something or feel something. There is no reason we should know it; we simply do. Many people are reluctant to admit they "hear voices" for fear of sounding crazy, but everyone who has heard the spirits attests to how perfectly natural it is. In fact, seldom do we need to be taught to do this; we just do it. Speaking to the dead, and hearing their replies, is simply another side of human nature.

An interesting insight from spiritual traditions around the world, and one found in folktales and mythology, is that spirits have a corresponding need to contact us. It is not just the recently departed spirit who seeks to return and check up on things, but the spirit folk in general reach out to us. What I call the "spirit folk" are perceived differently in different cultures and spiritual traditions. They might appear as fairies, little people, gods and goddesses, earth spirits, animal powers, saints, angelic beings—and, more recently, the extraterrestrials who visit our planet. It is not always clear what the spirit folk need from us, but the fact that they need us is universally recognized.

For example, in the Judeo-Christian tradition, angels and saints ask mortals to undertake sacred missions. In Celtic legends the fairy folk lure humans into the otherworld to marry them and have children. In Native American tradition, animal spirits will remain loyal guardians, even for people who don't cooperate with them. In nature-oriented cultures the spirits of the land, the forest, the fields, and the crops demand that human beings conduct seasonal rituals to assure fertility, a bountiful harvest, and plentiful food. The implication in all of these instances is very interesting: we live in a cooperative universe, where mortals and immortals, humans and nonhumans, the living and the dead are partnered in the great dance of Creation. We need each other; none can dance it alone.

Spirits require human effort, human companionship,

a mutual partnership *with us*. Wherever we look, we find that spirits on the other side approach us in the hopes of establishing some type of relationship. Throughout the ages people have honored the spirits' requests: they have accepted sacred missions, traveled to the realms of the otherworld, honored animal guardians, and joyfully celebrated the fertile gifts of nature. This mutual need between mortals and spirits is as old as Creation.

What we think of today as a typical seance—a table, a medium, a circle of sitters, a dimly lit room—has been popular for only about 150 years. This book will focus primarily on the seance as it has evolved over the last century or so, but the theories and practices discussed here can be adapted and applied to situations that do not fit the classic seance. Be bold and experiment. Discover your own personal methods for communicating with the spirits. Let the world of the spirits become part of your own world, enriching it and you. As Walt Whitman might say, you will find your horizons expanding onward and outward, nothing collapses, and you will discover that death—and the spirits of the dead—are different from what you now suppose. And luckier.

↤ 3 ↦
BECOMING A MEDIUM

IN 1977 RESPIRATORY THERAPIST Remy Chua began having dreams about a co-worker who had been brutally murdered two weeks earlier. Chua first saw the slain nurse, whose name had been Teresita, while she was sleeping in the locker room at the hospital where they had both worked; when Chua opened her eyes, she saw Teresita standing in front of her as if she were still alive. Afterward Chua started to have dreams in which she witnessed the murder. In time she was convinced, from what she saw in her dreams, that the murderer was Allan Showery, an orderly at the hospital. Eventually Chua's dreams and trances became vocal, and Teresita, who was, like Chua, a Filipina, spoke through Chua in Tagalog, a native language in the islands. Teresita confirmed that the orderly had indeed murdered her, and she asked her friend to tell the police. Chua's husband, who was in bed beside her, heard the message.

When the Chuas decided not to go to the police, Teresita continued to appear to Remy and gave her evi-

dence so she could present a convincing case: she said that
Showery had stolen some jewelry from her and given it to
his girlfriend. Teresita also gave Remy the phone number
of her cousins, who could identify the jewelry. The Chuas
then went to the police. Investigators discovered that Showery had indeed given his girlfriend some jewelry shortly
after the murder. Theresita's cousins identified the jewelry,
and eventually Showery confessed to the crime. He was
sentenced to fourteen years in prison. The incident received widespread media attention.

SPONTANEOUS MEDIUMSHIP

Remy Chua's case, in which she served as a medium for
Teresita to help solve her own murder from the other side,
is a classic example of spontaneous or involuntary mediumship. Quite a few people experience spontaneous mediumship, although usually on a less dramatic scale and
without the publicity. We will never know how many
ordinary people have spontaneous mediumship experiences. A common scenario is that shortly after death a
friend or loved one appears, usually for some specific
purpose. The appearance or communication may occur
while we are dreaming, or in the hypnagogic state that
occurs shortly before falling asleep, or even fully awake
(but usually going about some routine task or in a reflective
state of mind).

Involuntary mediumship often startles people, thrust-
ing them into a role they know little about. Many people
never ask to be mediums, and they prefer that the deceased stay on the other side and leave them alone. As a
matter of fact, involuntary and spontaneous contacts with
the dead can be extremely disruptive of normal living and
particularly disturbing to people who don't have strong

beliefs in the afterlife or the possibility of communication between the worlds of the living and the dead. Such contacts force unbelievers to consider that their paradigm of the universe might be inaccurate or incomplete. For them, life may never be the same again.

Nevertheless, many mediums have discovered their talent to contact or be contacted by spirits quite unexpectedly. But as long as their talent remains sporadic and unintentional, they are not very reliable mediums. They need to be able to reach out to the spirit world if they want to serve as the channel for meaningful communications. This means they must learn to control their trances, so they go into them and come out of them intentionally. Only from practice and experience will they learn how to evaluate the quality of spirit communications, discern accurate information, reject bogus messages, and help clients interpret obscure statements.

What Are Mediums Like?

It's surprising to discover how ordinary mediums are. They live in houses with backyards that need cutting, shop for groceries at local supermarkets, have children and grandparents, go to churches or synagogues, get headaches and take aspirin, watch television, go on vacations. Most also hold down average jobs and worry about paying bills. Mediums can be found just about anywhere on the scale of human interests and personal characteristics, just like the rest of humanity.

A romantic stereotype of the medium or psychic, however, has been ingrained into our imaginations through literature and movies. Namely, mediums are somewhat cranky, eccentric misfits who stumble through life, leaving a trail of psychic chaos wherever they go. Undoubtedly such psychics exist, and most people know one or two individuals, whether psychically gifted or not, who fit the description. Some mediums consciously present themselves as bizarre, mysterious, ethereal beings, hoping that their images will drum up business. Others are already in the limelight and cater to their audiences' and followers' desires to have a source of mystery and magic in their lives. But the glamorous mediums are the exception. Most mediums live rather ordinary lives and appear no different from anyone else.

Mediums do, however, tend to display some unique characteristics not shared or appreciated by people whose lives are more fully focused on this world rather than the invisible worlds. Mediums live in both worlds and develop an acute sensitivity to spirit activity. Since spirits are around us all the time, mediums may be more aware of them as a constant presence in their lives. This is not to say that the medium cannot function in his or her ordinary life because of spirit distractions. To the contrary, the medium is better qualified to live successfully on this plane precisely *because* the medium knows what is going on. It is the untrained, unsuspecting person who is more likely to be unsettled by spirit activity. The nonmedium often experiences the spirits as vague fears, or unexplained changes in mood, or startling synchronicities that threaten the commonly accepted view of reality. We are all constantly living in more than one reality, for the simple reason that the universe is made up of many realities. The person who knows this and accepts it and understands how to function within multiple realities has an advantage over someone who does not.

Synchronicities are a case in point. A synchronicity is a meaningful coincidence that seems to defy the law of cause and effect. Anyone who begins to practice a serious spiritual or psychic life experiences synchronicities that previously went unnoticed or were written off as "just weird coincidences." The truth is that synchronicities happen to us every day, because that is the way the universe operates. Creation is a great web of interrelationships. Tugging on any strand in the web sends vibrations in all directions. Everything is connected to everything else. So it is not surprising to be thinking about a friend who then phones you within minutes, or to dream of someone's illness a week before it occurs, or to be in need of a certain book and have it suddenly fall off a shelf practically into your lap. Events like these occur more often than we think. The universe does these sorts of things all the time to wake us up to the realization that we are not alone or isolated from the rest of creation. But to people who are not aware of the psychic dimensions of the universe, these things seem to be rare and happen with regularity only to "crazy mediums and offbeat psychics."

The personality most suited to successful mediumship is not the high-strung, overly sensitive, thin-skinned one, but one that exudes peace, relaxation, calm, and an openness to whatever is. An open, nonjudgmental mind and heart are paramount. In fact many mediums insist that the heart is more important than the mind, even though the popular impression is that mediumship is mind work. The best mediums are simple, open-hearted, clear-minded men and women who can stop and "enter the silence" within themselves and receive the wisdom and knowledge of the universe.

It also surprises some people to learn how many mediums lead deeply religious lives and pray regularly to know the Divine Will and follow It in their daily lives. The great twentieth-century medium Arthur Ford once said that he didn't know anyone who prayed regularly for these intentions who did not develop some means of extrasensory awareness. It is not uncommon for mediums to begin a seance with a short prayer to God, the Divine Spirit, the Great Mystery, or All-That-Is for assistance.

TRANCE

Very few spirit contacts occur without some type of altered state shaping the consciousness of the person who sees or hears the spirits. The word *trance* is the most common term for this altered state of awareness, but we should define the term carefully.

There are many types of altered states of consciousness. The phrase *altered state* itself can be misleading to many people who associate it exclusively with LSD trips, comas, drunkenness, and other extreme forms of nonordinary consciousness. Out-of-body experiences and hypnotism also require a change of consciousness, as do such everyday acts as dreaming, daydreaming, mindless reverie, and the mesmerizing stare that overcomes many drivers on boring interstate highways. In fact, if you close your eyes and breathe deeply for as little as two minutes, your brain waves change and you alter your ordinary state of consciousness.

Altered states of awareness are common human facilities. There is nothing supernatural or bizarre about them, other than that they are not the style of consciousness in which we go through most of our daily activities. They seem unfamiliar to most people because our society generally discourages private visionary experiences in favor of mass-produced fantasies such as movies, video games, and comic books. Other societies, especially tribal, nature-oriented societies, encourage visionary work and virtually all, male and female, young and old, are expected to have visionary experiences that bring them into contact with the invisible worlds.

We should take special notice of illness as a spiritual opportunity. During times of sickness our normal ego restrictions are severely threatened. We feel particularly vulnerable because we are literally "not ourselves," not "feeling up to our usual selves." However we phrase it, we are in an altered state of existence, one in which we may be exceptionally receptive to spirit influences. Spiritualists value very highly the visions that skeptical materialists might write off as "hallucinations" (usually described as "raving"). Sometimes the greatest spiritual insights and leaps in our spiritual development occur when we are most physically debilitated.

What type of consciousness is necessary for mediumship? From accounts of mediums themselves, it appears that all of those just mentioned can work. Some mediums "go under" completely and recall nothing of what takes place in the room while they are in trance. Their ordinary awareness shuts down, and they become totally focused on their visitation with the spirits. At the other end of the spectrum are mediums who maintain a strong awareness of where they are and what they are doing and who are able to perceive the invisible worlds while functioning in ordinary reality. They might even be able to crack a personal joke with a sitter while channeling information from a spirit.

"Going into trance," the phase most commonly used, is a personal experience that varies from medium to medium. If you have never gone into trance, you will have to discover the techniques that work best for you, and explore your nonordinary state of consciousness so that it becomes familiar and comfortable. Approach this work with an open mind and don't rely too heavily on what you may have heard or read is the "best" or "only" way to shift your awareness.

Learning to achieve an altered state of consciousness at will is important for anyone hoping to communicate with the dead. Once you have mastered this skill and are comfortable with it, you'll be able to move between the worlds with ease.

Discovering Your Style of Visionary Consciousness
Here is an easy, safe technique for discovering the style of trance or nonordinary state of consciousness that you can use in mediumship.

Begin by sitting comfortably, feet on the floor, hands lying loosely in your lap or on a table. Close your eyes and take four or five deep, slow, complete breaths. Your stomach should expand on the complete inhale and contract at the peak exhale, but do not strain or hold your breath. Let it flow rhythmically and smoothly.

Focus your attention on your breathing, noting the top and bottom of each breath, that is, the full state of inhalation and the empty state of exhalation. Gradually you will become less aware of your physical environment and more attuned to your own inner states and to the timeless-placeless condition that results from observing the repeated cycle of breaths. If it takes more than four or five full breaths to achieve this state, simply continue breathing until you become aware of it. You may need to practice this for several days before you recognize the shift in consciousness.

As with other human talents, some people learn to shift consciousness quickly, others more slowly. It's possible that you will go into a light trance immediately and without much warning. (Remember throughout this book that we are using the word *trance* in a very broad sense to mean any nonordinary state of awareness; it does not imply a total loss of awareness.) Some people experience bodily jerks or twitches as they go into trance, while others slide into the altered state smoothly and imperceptibly. There are also two somewhat opposite sensations that you may experience. One is a heaviness or sleepy feeling; the other is a lighter and more alert feeling. Odd though it sounds, you may even experience them simultaneously, feeling sleepy because you are turning off the distracting stimuli in the environment around you while you also become more alert and sensitive to the invisible world of nonordinary reality, the spirit realms.

Do not make quick judgments about what is happening to you. A critical mind is the ordinary state of consciousness that you want to turn off temporarily. Observe and witness the changes in your awareness but do not judge them. You can reflect on them or analyze them later.

To leave the state of nonordinary consciousness, let your attention move away from your breathing by listening to sounds around you or noticing the temperature of the air in the room or a breeze. Gradually become aware of where you are sitting, the chair beneath you, your feet on the floor. Take a few more relaxed breaths and open your eyes.

SPIRIT GUIDES

Many mediums credit whatever wisdom, insight, or power they have to helping spirits, the guides who teach us and the guardians who protect us. Sometimes the guide and guardian is the same spirit, but it is not uncommon for a person to have several or even many helping spirits, each specializing in different activities or kinds of information. Spirit guides may be deceased relatives, more ancient ancestors, human figures who are not related to you, angelic beings who have never been incarnated, spirits from other universes who have never had a material existence, or animal spirits.

Some spirit guides are what many people today refer to as *light beings*. Light beings may not have any recognizable shape, or they may look vaguely human or animal or a combination. Their forms may take different shapes on different occasions. In general they appear as radiant, light-filled, or light-emanating centers that seem warm, supportive, friendly, and compassionate. Most people who have survived NDEs report having seen these light beings before they returned.

In classical seance terminology, the guide is often called the *control* or *contact* through which the medium receives communications from other spirits. A control might call the spirits, invite them to the seance, and introduce them to the medium and sitters. Just as the medium is the go-between for the living and the dead, the control or spirit guide is the go-between for the medium and the spirit world.

As we noted earlier, the guide may simply summon a spirit and allow the spirit to talk to the medium, or the guide may act as interpreter for the spirit and medium and do all the talking. You will have to discover how your own guide intends to work.

Arthur Ford, the prominent medium mentioned earlier, worked with a guide named Fletcher, who was the spirit of a young French Canadian boy who had been a playmate of Ford's for a while during Ford's childhood in Florida. Fletcher was killed in action during World War I. Ford's method of going into trance was to breathe deeply and visualize Fletcher's face. Ford saw Fletcher more clearly on each inhalation, giving him the sensation that he was breathing the spirit of his guide into him. Eventually

Ford felt that his face and Fletcher's face had merged, that he and Fletcher had become one. At that point Ford knew he was in trance and could begin channeling messages.

Psychologist Carl Jung met an old man whom he called Philemon in one of his visionary, dreamlike experiences. For Jung, Philemon represented the wisdom of the ages and was Jung's personal link with universal knowledge. The famous twentieth-century psychic Eileen Garrett had two guides in the course of her career. One was the spirit of an Arab named Uvani, who lived in the previous century. The other was Abdul Latif, a Persian physician whose last incarnation on earth was in the thirteenth century.

Spirit guides and controls are often individuals with whom we have a natural rapport, someone with similar interests or attitudes toward life. After all, you have to work together, and your guide can become an ongoing part of your life, both in and out of trance, so you might as well have something in common besides an interest in seances. A true guide respects your autonomy and independence, however, and never "possesses" you in the sense of taking over your mind or body so that you lose your identity. Even though the guide is referred to as the control, *you* are always in control, and your guide knows and respects that. He or she is an assistant for a special type of spiritual work, not a dictator to run your ordinary life.

Mediums assure us that the same types of personality attract, even between the worlds. Therefore, if you have positive intentions and are a good person, so are your guides. Like attracts like. You need not fear that some disrespectful or malicious spirit will enter your consciousness or "take over" and tempt you to do things you would not do in ordinary consciousness. As Arthur Ford put it, "The pure in heart are safe, and those truly devoid of self-interest find unseen collaborators of the same sort."

The Nature of Spirit Guides

This brings us to the interesting question, raised by many people over the last 150 years, as to whether the medium's guide is a separate entity or simply some part or aspect of the medium's personality. Is the guide a separate being, or is it really part of the medium's higher self? Some researchers and psychics suggest that the guide is a part of the medium's personality that is more fully aware of the invisible realms, an area in the psyche tuned into the greater universe.

In Jungian terms the guide may be thought of as an archetype plugged into the collective unconscious, where contact with other psyches and spirits takes place naturally and as a matter of course. In this sense the guide is a part of the medium's soul that appears in a certain shape and form. It may even be a more remote or deeper part of the soul that cannot manifest while we are in ordinary consciousness (because ordinary consciousness acts as a kind of filter to keep our attention focused on ordinary reality, where we have to live our daily lives). The purpose of the guide is to loosen the normal ego controls over awareness, to allow deeper spiritual truths to surface into consciousness, to reveal hidden knowledge that is available to us but screened out during most of the day. Put another way, the guide is a function of the medium's personality that allows the medium to overcome self-consciousness and become aware of the spirit world.

Mediums themselves are not always certain just who or what the guide is. Arthur Ford did not mind if people thought Fletcher to be just another part of Ford's mind, as long as they recognized that Fletcher (whatever his nature) was a true channel of information from the spirit world to the world of the living. It has been argued that, since we are all one anyway, in a cosmic sense, it does not matter if an entity is separate from us. What is most important, certainly, is that the perception of "different beings" can be of great use and comfort to us on this plane.

Spirit Guides from Ancient Cultures

Many contemporary mediums and channelers have spirit guides who were last incarnated in ancient or native societies, such as Native American medicine men and women or tribal shamans from Peru or Siberia. Druids from the Celtic tribes of Western Europe and wizards of various archaic cultures are also prevalent. Why are there so many guides from the so-called " primitive" cultures?

Anthropologists and ethnographers note that ancient people were more psychically attuned to the spirits of nature than we are because their lives were more intimately bound up with the cycles of nature on a daily basis. They were more sensitive to trees, animals, the landscape, seasons, and the elements—in other words, to Creation and to the Spirit of Creation. Our ancestors recognized spirits in all living things. Since their everyday life was richly spirit-filled, their own spirits, now in the next world, are greatly evolved in ways to communicate between the various worlds and forms of life. Put simply, ancient people were more psychic and spiritually sensitive while they were alive on earth, and they continue to be so in the spirit world. They are also interested in helping modern Westerners reclaim their lost visionary powers.

Ancient people seem to have had no doubts about the next life and the continuation of personality after death. For the most part they did not fear death as so many modern people do. If medicine people, shamans, and wizards are returning in great numbers to serve as spirit guides for modern people, it might be to share with us their strong belief in the afterlife and their awareness of the spirit world that characterized their earthly lives. Such attitudes may be the exact corrective for us who try to deny the reality of death and to repress our "intimations of immortality."

Meeting Your Guides

There are various ways to meet your spirit guides. One of the most powerful and convincing ways is to ask your guide to come to you in your dreams at night. You may have to request this for several nights in a row. It may take a week or more, particularly if you are not good at remembering your dreams. Begin to record your dreams, if you do not already, and notice who appears in them. A spirit guide will not be someone still alive. It may, however, be a deceased relative or ancestor, an animal, or a human figure whom you have never met before. After meeting your guide in a dream, you can use the method of going into trance described earlier (or the method of spontaneous writing explained later in this chapter) and begin to get to know your guide. Begin with the following questions.

- What is your name? (Or, what do you want to be called?)
- What lives have you lived on earth, if any?
- Where do you come from?
- How do you want to work with me?
- What methods should I use to contact you?
- Can you introduce me to any other spirit guides that would be helpful for me to meet at this time?

If you do not meet a guide in dreams, use this mediational approach. Sit comfortably and shift your consciousness as described earlier. See yourself sitting in a safe, comfortable place outdoors. Ask your spirit guide to come up and stand behind you. Wait until you feel its presence. Then slowly turn around, in your mind's eye, and look at the ground so that you first see the guide's feet. Then gradually raise your gaze and proceed up to the face, noticing how the guide is dressed, the colors and textures of clothing, and so forth. (If the spirit has an animal form or is an angelic being, it will not look human, but you can address it as you would a spirit with a human form.) When you reach the face, look confidently into his or her eyes and say, "Hello, my name is [X]. What is your name?"

You need not go through the entire meditation at one sitting. If you feel you want to meet your guide more gradually, stop after you feel its presence behind you and tell it you will come back later. At the second session you may want simply to turn around and see your guide but not speak. In the third session you can begin the dialogue. Proceed at the pace that seems right for you.

Some people report that they see the body and clothing of their spirit guides very clearly, but the face always seems vague or poorly defined, without any clear features. Sometimes the figure is hooded and the face is never quite visible. There is a universal belief that some spirits are too evolved or perfected for us to look at directly. This may be the case with a spirit guide whose face is never quite visible. You may have a strong desire to see the face clearly, since the face is the most expressive part of the human body and we recognize someone and get to know someone through his or her face. You may feel disoriented at first if you cannot see your spirit guide's face, but in time you will get used to it. It is also possible that you are not ready to see it at this time and that the guide will show you his or her face later.

When you do begin to communicate, ask the questions just listed. Let the conversation and amount of information your guide gives you flow naturally and spontaneously. You need not ask all the questions or try to learn everything you want to know in one session. In fact you are just beginning a long-lasting relationship, so go slowly. What is important is that you meet each other consciously and develop a pattern of contact, through either dreams, meditation, trance sessions, spontaneous writing, or some other method you work out together.

TYPES OF SPIRIT COMMUNICATION

There are three basic types of communications experienced by mediums: sentient, auditory, and visual. Usually each medium feels more comfortable with one type of contact than the others, but it is not uncommon for a medium to channel messages from the spirits in more than one way, or to experience some combination of communication methods. There are also times when one method may be more effective than the others, given time, place, and the inclinations of the medium, client, or spirit. As a medium you should be familiar with all three types, for each is an important window into the spirit world.

Sentient messages are "felt" rather than heard or seen. The sentient medium "feels" what the spirit is saying, receives impressions or the general drift of ideas and tunes in to the basic theme of the message. This form of communication is similar to thought transmission, in which one person places a thought, or the core of a thought, into the mind of another. A sentient medium then "translates" or "interprets" the thought or message into his or her own words to share it with others. In some respects sentient messages are intuited, although practically speaking, intuition is involved in all three types of spirit communications. Beginners often experience sentient messages at first, sometimes (though not always) later receiving auditory and visual messages as well.

An audient medium "hears" voices. The messages are audible to the medium, although possibly not to others in the room. The medium can then relay the exact words he or she hears to others, or the message may be put into the medium's own words. Sometimes the medium hears only a few words or snatches of a message, or a phrase or key sentence, which require some elaboration and interpretation to make sense. The medium then "fills out" the message so that it successfully communicates what the spirit intends.

Both audient and sentient messages can be spoken or written out by the medium. We will look at spontaneous writing in greater detail in the next section.

A visual medium "sees" spirits. As with voices, the visual image of the spirit may not be perceptible to others in the room. A visible spirit is called an *apparition*. It may speak in a way that is audible to everyone or just a select few. In some cases, even though the spirit's mouth is moving, only the medium or some specific person in the circle can hear the words.

Seeing spirits is never necessary for mediumship. In some ways it is frosting on the cake. Most spiritualists and psychic investigators believe that it is up to the spirit to decide whether he or she wants to be visible to the living. The energy required for a spirit to appear visibly is probably greater or more complex than that needed for merely communicating messages, and spirits may not always be able to, want to, or need to appear.

WRITING MEDIUMSHIP

Automatic writing is one of the easiest and most convenient techniques for developing skills as a medium. Writing may not prove to be the best or most natural method for you later on, when you become more self-confident, and it may not be the method your guide prefers to use with you, but it is a particularly effective means for discovering and practicing mediumship skills. Writing is also an effective way to meet and get to know your spirit guide if you do not yet know who your guide is.

Writing is a good place to start because when we sit with a blank piece of paper in front of us and a pen in hand, we naturally seem to fall into a dreamlike state of consciousness. There is something mysterious and alluring about the emptiness of a blank sheet of paper and the realization that with a pen or pencil you can create pictures, words, or graphic designs at will or out of your subconscious reservoir of memories, dreams, and visions. Sitting in front of a blank sheet of paper is like being perched on the brink of creation with total freedom to bring into being whatever you desire.

Begin with the breathing exercises described in the earlier section "Discovering Your Style of Visionary Consciousness" until you feel relaxed and peaceful. Open your eyes and look at the paper. Rest the pencil (or pen) loosely on the paper to lessen resistance. Some mediums suggest that you hold the pencil in some way other than your customary position and not rest your hand on the paper. This sends a message to your subconscious that you are not merely sitting down to write a letter or shopping list; something out of the ordinary is about to take place. This measure is optional, however, especially if holding the pencil in an unfamiliar manner is clumsy or cramping. You definitely do not need to hold the pencil differently throughout the seance. Once the writing begins, you can adjust the pencil to your normal writing style.

If this is your first attempt to achieve a trance state

and meet your spirit guide, begin with a short, heartfelt invocation stating your intention. It may be as simple as "Whoever you are that is with me, I wish to meet you." If you already know your guide, bring its presence into your consciousness and announce your intention to communicate with it or any spirit willing to begin a beneficial dialogue with you at this time. Don't ask for a specific spirit other than your spirit guide in these early practice sessions. The goal here is not to contact a particular individual but to develop your skills at making contact and receiving messages from the spirits through writing.

You may have to sit quietly and wait for a few moments. When your guide or another spirit is present, you will feel the urge to move the pencil on the paper. You may even experience a trembling or shaking in your arm and hand. It may feel as if something or someone is pulling your hand across the paper. These are signs that spirits may be present. In whatever way you experience this tug or urge to write, you'll know that it is time to begin putting letters, words, phrases, or drawings down on paper.

The first marks on the paper may be disappointing scratches or doodles, traces of letters, odd meaningless designs, or just scribbles. Sometimes this is part of the "warming up" process before the actual words begin to appear. Do not resist this stage or give up, but stay with it until words finally appear.

As your hand moves the pencil over the page, your heart and mind may be actively engaged as well. In other words, as the pencil makes markings, words, and phrases, feelings or ideas may occur simultaneously, and you will feel drawn to let your hand express them further in words, pictures, or graphics. Often the communication begins this way, with your mind, heart, and hand working together. Sometimes your mind and hand will cooperate throughout the entire session. At other times you may notice that nothing in particular is passing through your mind, that no particular feelings well up in your heart. Everything goes blank, as it were, and the spirit moves your hand independently of the rest of your body or mind. You may even feel something like a "split" mind effect, in which you are actively thinking about something unrelated to the messages appearing on the page.

In most sessions, however, you will become consciously or semiconsciously involved in dialogue with the spirits, asking questions, receiving answers, and remaining aware of the communications that appear on the page. If you have sitters, you will hear their questions.

In the initial sessions, whether alone or with sitters, ask simple yes-or-no questions at the start. Avoid frivolous and even personal questions at first. Your goal is to make contact with a spirit, learn its identity, and develop a relationship. Since like attracts like, you may discover that the spirit has interests similar to your own and that one of the reasons a particular spirit wants to meet you and work with you is that he or she can instruct or counsel you along lines that are in the spirit's own field of interest or expertise. This is especially true of spirit guides.

If you seem to be getting nothing but gobbledgook or silly messages that make no sense, and you suspect that a frivolous, jokester spirit has appeared, call on your guides to send him or her away and bring someone more serious. It's best not to indulge the "silly" spirits just to achieve contact. You don't want to establish a reputation in the spirit world as a medium who enjoys the company of pranksters and cranksters. Mediumship is a serious undertaking, not a parlor game. You are not performing to entertain your guests or sitters.

Patience, concentration, openness, and a sense of detachment are necessary each time you sit down to work. You have to be willing to accept the fact that no one may come on any given occasion. If after ten or fifteen minutes you don't feel the presence of spirits and your hand seems to refuse to write, stop for the moment and try again later. Sometimes just taking a break for a half hour, going for a walk, or enjoying some herbal tea is enough. Sometimes we are blocked without really knowing why, and a short distraction will unblock us. And sometimes it is the spirits who are not ready.

As mentioned earlier, time and place are not the same for spirits as they are for us. Nor can we always (if ever) understand *their* sense of time and place. We may never be able to figure out why a spirit can visit us at 5:30 but not at 5:00, but that is not for us to worry about. (You can always ask, of course, but the spirits may not answer or not answer to your satisfaction.) We just have to accept the fact that spirits are involved in the greater universe in ways we will never quite appreciate while we are still in our bodies. In other words they are busy; they have more to do than be at our beck and call, even when they have expressed interest in us and we have an ongoing relationship with them.

If you have been receiving messages consistently and then they seem to fade, the spirit may be leaving. Mediums can generally sense when spirits are "signing off" and when they are just "taking a break." In time you will recognize the difference clearly. Spirits tend to give some sign of farewell or say good-bye, but not always. At the start, go with your instincts if you think a session is over. But be open to the possibility that a spirit is merely pausing for some reason. Continue to sit with the pencil resting lightly on the paper, waiting for possible further communications.

Practice writing mediumship every day if you are

INTERFERENCE

John uses automatic writing for his medium work. His method consists of writing out full messages from the spirits and/or using a word or phrase as a trigger to give him the intent of the message, which he feels in his heart and then speaks out loud; he usually begins speaking the spirits' communications when they are coming too fast for him to write. He has several friends who sit with him regularly, but he also allows guests to join them, usually people who have specific questions or hope to make contact with a particular spirit. John's spirit guide, Allan, often answers people's questions if they are of a general nature about life, death, and the afterlife. When a person wishes to contact a specific spirit, Allan calls that spirit, introduces him or her to John, and then John's writing reflects that spirit's direct communication.

One evening the seance was proceeding smoothly as John wrote out messages from several spirits that showed up, including the deceased uncle of Sandy, a young woman present for the first time. Sandy asked a few questions of her uncle, which he answered forthrightly. The man had died twenty years before, so she was not in any great distress over contacting him. But as John wrote, the word grief *appeared in the middle of the sentences where it didn't make any logical sense. Eventually, each time John began writing an answer to a new question,* grief *was the first word to appear, and John could write nothing beyond it. John himself began to grow sorrowful, and he felt a strong grieving sensation in his chest.*

John paused and told the circle not to ask any more questions for a few moments. Then he said to them, "Allan says that someone here tonight is grieving for a deceased relative." No one responded. John rephrased the statement,

"Is anyone here grieving for someone?" No one answered yes, but Chuck, one of the evening's guests, said that he was feeling sad about a friend who was dying of cancer. John's hand wrote yes, a confirmation from Allan.

Then John asked Chuck if he had been worrying about the friend that evening. *"Yes,"* Chuck answered. *"When Sandy's uncle appeared, I started to think of my friend, and I just couldn't get him out of my mind."* John explained to Chuck that when an extremely strong emotion possesses a sitter it can interfere with spirit communications. One way to think of it is that the emotion weakens the group's focus and thins out the receptive energy the spirits are using to speak to the medium. Another explanation is that the medium may be picking up the most powerful emotion or obsession present at the table. Either way, Chuck's presence became an impediment to successful spirit communication.

John asked Chuck to sit outside the circle or wait in the next room until his worries about his friend subsided, and then rejoin the group if he felt up to it. Once Chuck removed himself from the actual group around the table, the spirit messages flowed through John and his guide as before. Later, after the circle took a break for refreshments, Chuck rejoined them, and there was no further interference.

serious about developing your sensitivity to spirit contact. Just ten or fifteen minutes is enough. Many professional mediums continue to practice automatic writing throughout their lives. The spirits and guides often use these quiet practice sessions to encourage and instruct us in mediumship work. It is also important for mediums to remain humble and thankful for the gifts they have. Approaching the spirits in practice sessions is a way of acknowledging your dependence on them and your small role in the greater scheme of things.

In your first practice sessions you may feel awkward and self-conscious. You may have strong doubts about the whole thing. Don't let this worry you. Faith is not necessary. Sometimes skeptics who practice automatic writing discover that the spirits can use them as effectively as believers. In fact, occasionally a true believer will not be able to receive messages. Belief is not a diploma for mediumship; it does not remove the blocks that can prevent us from opening up to the invisible worlds around us. For many reasons, often unknown to us, spirits do not communicate through someone just because that person believes in them and wants to communicate.

Also avoid worry over whether the messages you receive are from the spirits or from your own unconscious (or even conscious) mind. It is normal for beginners to wonder about this. Am I just making it up, or is a spirit really speaking through me? In time this question will lose its importance as you learn to discern the difference between what is your own and what is from the spirits. You will also discover that some messages are a combination of your own thoughts and feelings and those of the spirits, and you'll realize that this is not always a problem. Sometimes the spirits need the medium's help in getting their ideas down on paper. That is why spirits tend to select mediums similar to them. A spirit or guide may in fact come to rely on your own intuitive sense of what needs to be said and inspire you with the general message, expecting you to put it in the proper words. If you are getting it "wrong," the spirit will usually let you know. You'll "hear" the correction or objection. At first, however, assume that the messages you are writing are from the spirits unless they tell you differently. And if they do, well, then *that's* the message!

Reaching Inward and Outward

Consciousness is a very elastic thing. You can expand it, deepen it, reshape it, tune it down or up. Consciousness is your tool for reaching inward and outward, *in* toward the depths of your own soul, *out* toward the farthest corners of the universe. The ability to shift consciousness can be learned and developed. The ordinary state of consciousness in which we spend most of our waking and working day is but one form of consciousness and usually the most dominant in our lives. In fact, for some of us ordinary consciousness is a tyrant, not allowing other modes of awareness to enrich the psychic texture of our lives. As you practice automatic writing, you will learn how to let your ordinary consciousness recede temporarily so that your everyday concerns fade from the forefront of awareness. Your ego will loosen up and your body relax.

It is vital to "soften" both body and ego so that neither is tense. A tense ego keeps the mind from receiving information other than your normal thoughts, fears, and truths. Your body, so interwoven with thought and feeling, will also block spirit information. If you imagine your body to be porous (as the cells and atoms that make it up actually are) and your ego boundaries to be equally diaphanous, you will be a more receptive medium. You need not fear becoming so porous that you dissolve or become flooded with alien entities. Your spirit guides protect you and act as screens to other spirits and any energies that might be harmful to you. Besides, most people, including mediums, have strong enough body and ego structures that they need not fear losing their identities.

Ideas, Symbols, and Images

In the mediumistic state of consciousness you will become sensitive to external and internal stimuli, developing the empathy to respond to imagery that conveys thoughts and feelings of the spirits who speak through you. For many intuitive mediums, the messages they convey to sitters arise out of the imagery the spirits give them. In other words, they don't hear exact words and sentences but gather images from the spirits. The medium may then have to "tease out" the meaning behind the imagery that will have some significance for the sitter.

George Anderson, a famous medium on Long Island who conducts his seances with pencil and paper, relates how important imagery is in his seances. His form of automatic writing is different from the usual methods in that he doesn't write out lengthy communications from the spirits but uses his writing as a form of concentration. He fills up his pages with words, names, and images, allowing the meanings behind these impressions to arise into his consciousness. For example, he may write the word *father* and tell the sitter that he is getting a "father vibration." The spirit speaking to him may not in fact be the client's father but a person who played that role in the client's life, a father figure such as a teacher or mentor, or even a grandfather. Anderson is wary of his tendency to interpret the symbols. It is normal to want to do so, and the sitter may ask what a particular symbol or word means. But the wise medium will be hesitant and let the symbols speak for themselves or let the spirits do the work. Too often an inexperienced medium will jump in too quickly and interpret a symbol incorrectly.

Some words and symbols may appear over and over in your writing. You may worry that this means you are making up the communications rather than receiving them from the spirits. But that is not always the case. Mediumship is like dream interpretation in that every medium, like every dreamer, develops a pool of symbols and images that have personal significance. George Anderson's pool of personal images are operas, films, television programs, books, famous personalities, and Catholic figures. You will discover your own images and the specific issues and concerns to which they refer. Knowing when to interpret an image symbolically, literally, or metaphorically requires patience and practice.

For example, you may receive an image of lying on a beach. If you interpreted that *literally*, you would tell the sitter that the spirit's message is about being on a beach, and this might be the case. The same image, interpreted *metaphorically*, however, might have nothing to do with going to the beach but be about relaxing, being outdoors, just getting away from the city. *Symbolically* the image of lying on a beach might have a particular meaning for you, such as childhood or summer. Be aware that many new mediums are inclined to take every image literally. Whenever an image comes through in a message, you must stay open to the possibility that the spirit is communicating something in an indirect fashion.

You must also be wary of attaching standard, popular associations to cultural symbols. A Christmas tree, for example, may not always be about the Christmas season. On a metaphorical level the tree may indicate something about rejoicing, celebrating, or being happy. As a symbol in your own repertoire of symbols and images, the tree may mean something personal to you, such as December or family life or something altogether unrelated to Christmas. The spirits tend to work with us on a very personal level, especially our guides, who sometimes know us better than we know ourselves. Over time you and your guides will discover or create the personal language and imagery that will make your seance work accurate and successful.

HYPNOTISM

Hypnotic trances can put a person in touch with past memories, previous lives, other universes, and the spirits of the dead. Why not use hypnotism then for seance work? In a sense, every time you create the visionary state of consciousness for a seance you are using a form of self-hypnosis. But deep hypnotic trances are not necessary for seance work and can even be a hindrance when the medium does not want to "go under" but to retain a certain level of awareness to interact with sitters. The accuracy of spirit communications does not depend on the depth of trance. Whatever works for a medium is what he or she should do.

Nevertheless, hypnotism can be an effective method for introducing a person to the visionary state of consciousness. A good hypnotist can train a person in visionary work by breaking down the barriers of perception so that the novice can have those important first experiences in another state of consciousness. In a hypnotic state, for instance, you can look back into your own past and reexperience events from your early life. Similarly, you may be able to go back into previous lives or contact other people who have now passed on and are in the spirit world.

Hypnotism can also create the altered state in which you first see spirits in the room or sense their presence. A hypnotist may help induce a trance and then ask you to look around the room and describe all the people who are present. As you scan the room, you may see the forms or shapes of spirits or detect concentrations of energy where spirits are present. In a hypnotic trance you might also meet your guide.

If you decide to use hypnotism to begin your training as a medium, select a reputable hypnotist whom you can trust. It is wise to ask for references to establish that a hypnotist has a credible reputation and isn't a fraud. Select someone well known in your community or among your friends. Explain why you want to be hypnotized and make sure that he or she is both sympathetic to your purpose and willing to use the trance sessions for the purpose of developing your own ability to work in an altered state of consciousness. Most important, you do not want to become dependent on the hypnotist or let the sessions get out of hand and wander off into areas that are of no interest to you. Keep your intention focused on the goal of becoming a medium.

SHARING A SPIRIT'S MESSAGE

There are two common methods of communicating a spirit's message to others: speaking and writing, either in the spirit's own words or in paraphrases created by the medium to explain the basic message. It doesn't matter whether the words, phrases, and jargon are the ones that the spirit usually used while in its last incarnation, as far as accuracy of communication is concerned, although these play an important role in establishing the identity of a spirit. (We will look at this issue of verifying a spirit's identity later on.) For the purpose of communicating, either the spirit's language or the medium's language will suffice, especially when you consider that a spirit might purposely change its speech patterns to make a particular message better understood. The exact words are not as important as the sense and meaning behind the communication.

The voice of a speaking medium may or may not sound like the former voice of the deceased. When the medium does capture the spirit's voice pattern and speech mannerisms, sitters are always more impressed, but the success of a seance does not hinge on this. Of course, the spirit's own characteristics may be important for convincing skeptical sitters that the spirit is really who it claims to be. It is not uncommon for a medium to begin a seance sounding very much like the deceased person and, as the seance progresses, to slip back into her or his natural speech patterns. This may have something to do with the amount or intensity of energy needed by the spirit and the medium to produce the spirit's voice; clearly, if communication without the spirit's former voice and speech characteristics requires less energy, the law of efficiency would suggest that we not expect to hear them. It always makes more sense to use the least amount of energy to accomplish a task.

The same considerations apply to foreign languages. Spirits may speak in their own languages through mediums who do not understand those languages. But it stands to reason that the easier, and possibly more accurate, approach is for the medium to convey the message in his or her own langauge so that it captures the sense and meaning of the spirit message, regardless of the language the spirit spoke while alive.

Some mediums never hear or receive messages directly from the spirits who visit a seance, but instead from the medium's personal spirit guide. Again, there are no hard and fast rules for this. Even when a medium usually relies on his or her guide, the guide might on some occasions step back, as it were, allowing the spirit to communicate directly with and through the medium.

PHYSICAL EVIDENCE

Unexplained physical activity often accompanies a seance. Noises, table tilting, scents or odors, breezes, changes in temperature, and similar phenomena may occur. A musical instrument in the room may play, or books may fall from a shelf, or some object in the room might float through the air. A physical object may materialize out of nowhere.

The spirits sometimes need to shake us out of our skepticism with some dramatic feat. Physical phenemona, while they can be dramatic and spellbinding, are in some sense the spirits' stage tricks to wake us up, get our attention, and establish their presence. Sometimes this is necessary. But for the sake of a successful seance, where the flow of communication between the living and dead proceeds unimpeded, flashy apparitions and poltergeistlike disturbances can become distractions. By themselves they often do not convey any meaningful communication. Obviously these events are awe-inspiring, but in many ways they are showmanship.

Stage magicians who enjoy debunking spiritualism take great pains to duplicate the physical phenomena that occur at seances on the assumption that, if a magician can perform the same feats, they must be tricks and the medium is therefore a fake—that is, a fake *medium*, not a fake magician! But it has been pointed out, over the last hundred or so years of psychical research and investigation, that a magician's ability to make a vase of flowers float off a table or an elephant appear in a room in no way discredits the truth of mediumship. There is more than one way to do just about everything. If magicians can perform these feats, so can spirits. And for the record, there have been physical phenomena at seances that were *not* stage tricks and that astounded even the professional magicians who tried and failed to reproduce them.

For example, the great stage illusionist Howard Thurston (who was one of the great fraud hunters of the early twentieth century), along with the famous Harry Houdini and Will Goldston (founder of the Magicians' Club of London), exposed many fake mediums. But on some occasions Thurston could not discover any fraudulent tricks for spirit phenomena. One evening he witnessed, in good light, a table rise in the air without the help of wires or other devices. He was convinced that it had levitated through the influence of spirits operating through the medium. Similarly, Will Goldston began his investigations convinced that 100 percent of all spirit phenomena was faked. After some twenty years he revised his figures, stating that he believed 80 percent was genuine and only 20 percent fake.

One medium I have worked with consciously avoids whatever appears to be, as she says, "hokey and dramatic," precisely because so many fraudulent mediums have perfected stage tricks to convince others of their powers. She believes that even working at a table, for instance, is a "setup for trickery." In her view, anything that makes a client wonder "How is the medium doing that?" detracts from the seance. By the way, even some of the genuine mediums have, on occasion, staged dramatic tricks to convince skeptical people or to enhance their reputations. Needless to say, hoaxes hurt the profession. A medium should be evaluated on how well and accurately he or she can contact spirits and convey messages in both directions, not on the physical phenomena that occur. So, aspiring mediums should not be intimidated by a lack of "special effects" at their seances.

Some mediums also suggest that the physical rappings and table tiltings that were common a century ago and in the early days of spiritualist practices were necessary because society was just beginning to discover, or rediscover, the possibilities of a continuing dialogue with the dead. The current age of materialism in the Western world required material proof that the spirits of the deceased were still around, and so the spirits used material means to make their point. Today physical spirit phenomena may be less common because we are a more believing, spiritually minded generation of mediums. We don't need the hardcore proofs that our great-grandparents did. At any rate, a new medium should not strive to duplicate the "great feats" of earlier mediums but should work to perfect his or her skills for making spirit contact and for accurately relating information that flows between the worlds of the living and the dead.

The most important training for mediumship comes from the spirits, not from books or lectures, which teach only techniques for developing our sensitivity to the spirit world and becoming more receptive to spirit contact. The truly great mediums learn their craft from their personal spirit guides and the spirits who instruct them during seances. A humble attitude, dedication to the work, and a continual willingness to practice and perfect your skills are all that you can really contribute. And no medium ever stops learning, for mediumship is a lifelong study.

↝ 4 ↜
THE CIRCLE

THE CIRCLE IS COMPOSED OF THE PEOPLE attending a seance, the *sitters*. The circle may include people who meet together regularly, as well as occasional guests and visitors. The sitters play an important role in creating the ceremonial space in which spirits feel free to make contact. In this chapter we will look at the group's role, the attitudes and responsibilities of individual members, problems that some people create in a circle, practical considerations like seating positions and organizational tasks, and how novices can start a development circle to get in touch with the spirit world.

Most people have lost contact with the spirits. But the world of the spirits has not lost contact with us, because it coexists side by side with our own world of ordinary reality. In the Celtic tradition there is a wonderful expression to indicate that the spirit world exists just beneath, inside, or on the other side of the terrain of ordinary reality: the Hollow Hills. In other words, nature is "hollow," containing an unseen fairy world of magic and mystery. Under the proper conditions, when the mist clears unexpectedly, when we turn around and find we have stumbled into a dream-like place, the two worlds open into each other, and travel and communication between them becomes possible.

The circle of sitters at a seance is one method of creating the conditions that facilitate the flow of energy between the visible and invisible realities. In fact a geometric circle is a universal, age-old symbol that people everywhere have associated with spiritual work. In many religious and esoteric traditions the circle is considered magical by its very nature because its seamless form has no beginning or end, no corners or sides, and every point is equidistant from the center. The circle, when properly cast or created, can be a place "between the worlds," a place that is neither here nor there.

This is not to say that contact with spirits cannot be made spontaneously or when you are alone. Far from it. Spirits come when they want, and competent mediums can communicate with spirit entities without the help of a group of people sitting in a circle. But the circle is a classic component of the traditional seance for a very good reason. It works. The community formed by people seated together in a circle for the express purpose of communicating with the spirits of the deceased acts as a catalyst for both the medium and the spirit.

THE GROUP AURA

Spirits are forms of energy, just as we are, but energy that is no longer concentrated within a physical body. Their energy is free-formed and free-floating. A spirit can be everywhere, or at least in several of our places at one time. It is not unheard of for the same spirit to speak to more than one medium or appear at several seances at the same time. The spirits incarnated centuries ago are still around also, as are those who will be incarnated years from now. Spirits from both the past and the future turn up at seances today. The qualities and the abilities of spirit energy are beyond our human, mortal understanding.

What does seem necessary, however, is for the spirit to make contact with a field of energy that is open and responsive to the spirit's overtures. The spirit's energy must contact some "terminal" in physical reality to make itself known and maintain a dialogue with an incarnate being. If it doesn't, the spirit's energy is like a breeze blowing aimlessly, without anything to catch or direct it. When passing through wind chimes on a porch or leaves of a tree, however, the breeze's energy becomes sound. Breath blown through a flute is transformed into musical tones. These analogies give us some insight into spirit energy. In a circle the spirit finds physical hearts and minds producing a field of energy where it can "link up" and express itself in ways that are perceptible to the living.

The group's energy field is composed of the individual fields of energy, or auras, surrounding each sitter at the seance. Although the human aura is not exactly physical, there are physical indications of how it operates. For example, every human body gives off heat, which can be felt within a certain radius around the body. Human bodies within a few feet of each other exchange water vapor after several minutes. The vibrations we radiate are so strong that many people instinctively pick up our feelings just by being in our presence. Occasionally we detect someone nearby before we actually see the person, such as when you get an eerie sensation walking down a street that someone in a window is watching you.

At a seance the separate auras of the sitters, highly tuned because of the spiritual work that unites them, merge into each other to create a group aura. This becomes the energy field on which a spirit imprints its messages, similar to the surface of film that is sensitive to light impressions. In other words, the pooled intentions and shared psychic energies create a sensitive environment where a spirit can imprint its thoughts and feelings.

In a sense the circle creates a common soul that gives life to the purpose of the group. The soul becomes a nucleus, a central source of energy that enlivens—or "enspirits"—the work. The group soul reaches out to the spirits, and they respond. In the circle they recognize a safe harbor where their needs and interests will be accepted. The soul of the circle has no fixed shape but is continually shifting and changing in response to the thoughts and feelings of the sitters. It is quite literally sensitive, like the film mentioned earlier, responding to the mental and emotional activity of the men and women in the circle and to the presence and communications from the spirits. For this reason it is critical that the sitters agree on their intention and purpose and work in harmony with each other.

HARMONY AND COOPERATION

The most effective attitude for sitters to have if they hope to create a successful circle is one of harmony and mutual cooperation. Once I attended a seance to make contact with a spirit that had been haunting a home, and the family who requested the seance allowed their teenage daughter and her friends to be part of the circle. The medium made no objection to this, and as the seance proceeded, it became clear that the younger members of the circle, who were all seated together at one end of the table, were not as focused as the older people. Occasional giggles and sighs of impatience indicated that the teenagers were more interested in themselves and what they were getting out of the evening than on helping the medium and the spirit in the house carry on a productive dialogue. Contact was made, and some useful communication took place, but the medium felt afterward that the seance was not very satisfying because of the "energy holes" in the circle created by the distraction of the younger sitters.

Wanting to be part of a seance is not a sufficient motive to create the finely tuned field of energy required for spirit contact. Each sitter must take responsibility for the success of the seance. No one in a seance circle is a passive observer. It would have been better for the teenagers to have sat outside the circle and watched, rather than take an active part.

Furthermore, the higher spirits have said that they will not come to a place of strife, chaos, or disharmony. Disruptive conditions can thwart a seance or attract the lower spirits that enjoy sowing disruption that reflects their own state of confusion.

We must meet the spirits halfway if we hope to have a successful seance. And that means recognizing that the spirits we wish to contact will be most comfortable in a milieu that re-creates the unity and oneness of the universe rather than one that emphasizes human individuality. Spirits, who realize the essential oneness of the human family, no longer contend with living "inside" the physical body, which for us is a constant reminder that we are in some sense separate from one another. The paradox of life, of course, is that even though we must live *as if* we are separate, individual beings (and in many respects we *are*), the deeper truth is that we are all part of the great Whole. We are not separate from the integrity of the universe. After crossing into the next life, we will have a more accurate view of this truth. When a spirit attends a seance, however, it must temporarily leave that realm of harmony and oneness and reenter, to some extent, our frustrating world of physical matter to communicate with us. It stands to reason that the more successfully a group of sitters re-creates the essential harmony and cooperative spirit of the universe within their small circle, the more willing the spirits will be to join them. And the easier it will be for them to do so.

Keep in mind that the sitters are not the only members of a circle. Each sitter is accompanied by his or her own spirit guides. The spirits are always present, even though our physical experience of time and space leads us to believe that they "come and go" (and for practical purposes we obviously find it necessary to speak of their coming and going). Each sitter brings personal spirit companions to every seance, and their energies also vibrate within the energy field of the circle and help to attract visiting spirits. By tuning in to your own helping spirits, especially the ones who serve as channels or teachers, you increase the harmonious environment of the circle. Visiting spirits communicate more freely and easily if they sense harmony, cooperation, and friendship among the sitters and their spirit guides. The overall group energy, both human and discarnate, must provide a receptive field for contact.

We each attract and bring spirits who are in sympathy with our deepest needs and aspirations, and in this respect each sitter exerts either a positive or a negative influence on the circle. If the circle is composed of highly ethical, tolerant, and compassionate human beings, the accompanying spirits will be the same. Since harmony and a cooperative spirit characterize the most effective circles, you should strive for a certain amount of homogeneity among your members. This doesn't mean that there cannot be a healthy and creative diversity, provided each individual's distinctive qualities are compatible with the overall tone and purpose of the circle. When they are not, meddlesome and cantankerous spirits have a greater chance for sowing discord among the members of the circle.

It is important for a group to understand and agree on the evening's purpose. Obviously the basic goal remains the same from session to session: to contact the dead and establish communication with them. But each seance has specific goals as well: to gather instructions about this life or the next, to learn more about the nature of the universe, to fulfill the last requests of someone who has recently departed, to make contact with a particular spirit. A session may be held to benefit a specific member of the group or to help a confused or frightened spirit. Or you may hold a healing seance for the entire group. Whatever your purpose, all members of the circle should agree to work constructively together. A member who cannot do so should sit out.

Curiosity is not a good group motive, although there may be one or two attendees (usually guests) who are there primarily out of curiosity. For example, it is usually best not to call in the spirits of the dead for information that can just as easily be obtained through some other form of divination, such as tarot reading, astrology, or a private channeling session.

Seances are forums for the greater communities of both the living and the dead to satisfy the mutual wishes and needs that bridge these worlds. Even when the seance is held to contact a specific friend or relative of one of the sitters, care should be taken to accommodate the needs of the spirit as well as the person at the table.

A small group is usually preferable to a large one. The smaller the group, the more clearly everyone can be in harmony with the evening's intention. The more people

present, the more chance for scattered intentions arising
from personal worries and concerns. Large groups can also
leave people feeling unsatisfied if for no other reason than
that they were just "part of the crowd" and did not realize
their contribution as clearly as they would have if the
group had been smaller. You will find the right number of
people for your circle, probably somewhere between five
and twelve individuals.

Negative Sitters

Some people should not be part of a seance because of the
intense negative energies they bring to it. There is no moral
judgment about this; even the best-intentioned individuals
might not be able to participate in a productive manner.
Through no fault of their own, they bring energy and a
spirit that is counterproductive.

For example, highly critical individuals usually cannot
"turn off" the running criticism in their minds to support
the group's goal. In one seance a woman who was a true
believer in the afterlife and the ongoing communication
between the living and the dead unwittingly charged the
circle with negative energy because she was continually
criticizing the way the circle was being run. She had something negative to say about how the sitters were positioned
around the table, whether the room was too bright or too
dim. She also complained incessantly about her chair
being uncomfortable. Although she was a personal friend
of many people in the circle, her discontent interfered with
the group's efforts to create a welcoming and tolerant
energy field for the spirits. Everyone has something to
complain about at some time or another, but if we find that
we just can't turn off our negative judgments, we will never
open our minds and hearts sufficiently to receive
the spirits.

Intently self-centered people also have a difficult time becoming part of the essential unity needed in a circle. For very legitimate reasons a person may be self-absorbed over the health of a loved one or financial problems, but these kinds of personal anxieties can interfere with a seance. Not only do they create a chaotic environment repellent to the higher spirits, but their strong, overpowering thoughts about themselves may be picked up by the medium and block his or her receptivity to spirit communications.

Curiously, skeptical people are not always bad sitters. A healthy skepticism can actually attract spirits who are interested in teaching unbelievers about the next life. Some mediums enjoy the challenge of having good-natured skeptics at their seances. But the skeptic should not express doubts before or during the actual sitting. Save them until the sitting is over. Questions and doubts should be discussed later, after the skeptic has time to think about the seance and put the evening's events into perspective. The atmosphere of the sitting should be one of agreement, cooperation, and confidence. Negative comments that in any way shake a medium's self-confidence or cast doubt on the work can be detrimental.

Obviously you should not invite openly hostile, close-minded, and argumentative people to a seance. Usually nothing that occurs at a seance will change their attitudes, and their energy tends to become overwhelmingly disruptive. You may want to work with these people privately if they are interested in learning more, but the sitting is not the place to do it.

A hypersensitive person can also be disruptive. Often this type of person claims to be "very psychic." Indeed these individuals are often finely attuned to psychic phenomena, but they don't know how to control and channel their sensitivity. At sittings they hear voices, see apparitions, get "strange feelings," and are flooded with spirit or psychic activity, but it confuses and sometimes frightens them. It is not for us to question whether the impressions they receive are legitimate. Whether real or imagined, the energy these individuals radiate does not contribute to the harmony of the circle.

Be aware of "psychic vampires" or "psychic sponges," who drain other people of their energy. They are often not bad or unprincipled people but usually are very needy, and they take every opportunity to replenish their store of spiritual or psychic energy. Sometimes a person will radiate an intensity, almost a hunger, for spiritual experiences that is not easy to ignore. It is not always clear whether that intensity comes from his or her store of energy, self-confidence, and knowledge or from a desperate need to fill an emptiness deep inside. While there is nothing wrong with the desire for fulfillment (we all seek it to some degree or other), many of these "intense" people are not team players and contribute nothing positive to the group energy. As you get to know these individuals, you will be able to evaluate them more effectively and will not be misled into thinking them likely candidates for the circle simply because of their interest in psychic phenomena. They need personal training to develop their own inner resources before they can participate constructively in a circle. A sitting requires people who will be at ease with the spirit world and spirit manifestations, not startled or overpowered by them.

It is important for the group to be able to screen out unwanted manifestations. Otherwise you might be inviting a cosmic free-for-all, an open invitation to any spirits who have nothing better to do. In a successful seance, even when you are not trying to contact a specific spirit and the invocation is somewhat open-ended, a common purpose will emerge once a specific spirit manifests and makes contact. At this point all the sitters should be able to focus their mediumistic faculties sufficiently.

The best attitude for sitters is to be open-minded, good-hearted, supportive, and helpful and to have a sense of humor. While seances are serious work, they need not be solemn. Spirits have a sense of humor too, and laughter is one of the human qualities that unites us. A fun remark, a lighthearted comment, and even a hearty laugh can unify a group and attract good-natured spirits. A laughing circle is usually a happy circle that anyone, whether in this world or the next, will find inviting.

The Dominant Sitter

Sometimes one or more sitters dominate a seance by being especially powerful transmitters or receptors.

A sitter actively dominates a seance as a *transmitter* when his or her thoughts and feelings permeate the group, even the medium's trance state. For example, a person greatly worried about the health of a family member may send out thoughts and feelings related to this, and, since everyone's psychic sensitivities are at a peak during a seance, other members in the circle pick up on them. The sitter's concerns may even unwittingly show up in messages from the spirits, since the way a medium presents a spirit message may be a combination of his or her own ideas and intuitions and the information relayed by the spirit. The fact that both conscious and unconscious thoughts from sitters can be projected into the stream of information passing through the medium is something that must be understood and faced.

Once a woman at a development circle (a circle that

meets for the express purpose of developing mediumistic skills) tried an experiment with a medium she thought was talking in vague generalities. The woman tried to project a thought to the medium to see if he picked up on it. She chose another member of the group and imagined that the grandmother of that member was trying to reach through to him. Sure enough, the medium began getting messages from the man's grandmother. Afterward the woman told the group what she had been doing. (Since the purpose of the group was experimental, they did not object to her "sabotage," because the group's goal was to study and experiment with all kinds of mediumistic phenomena.)

We need to be aware of all the possible influences at a seance and learn how to discern and evaluate them. If your own worries or obsessions seem to be feeding the communications at a seance, you should indicate that to the medium when the time seems appropriate, such as during a break or after the session ends. If the medium is not in a deep trance and is aware of what is going on around the circle, you could suggest to her or him that certain points in the communication might be coming from you. Some skeptics have suggested, in fact, that most or all of the information that comes through in a seance is via the medium's extrasensory perceptions; some people feel the medium simply reads the minds and lives of the sitters. Undoubtedly some information can come from these sources, but that does not rule out the possibility that other information is from the spirits. What's important is for a medium to be sensitive to all the influences and filter out those that are extraneous to the group's purpose.

A sitter dominates a circle as a *receptor* when the spirits talk directly to or through that sitter. A spirit may talk to more than one person at a seance and sometimes bypass the medium altogether. Spirits use the group's energy, so it is not unusual for one or more people within the group to be the primary energy focus for the spirit. Of course, if the spirit knows a particular sitter or has come with the express purpose of making contact with that sitter, the spirit could go directly to the person.

Often the type of people who attend seances are very open to spiritualist phenomena and may even have highly developed mediumship skills. When people predisposed to visionary experiences begin to receive messages, they usually are not startled by them. But someone who has never functioned as a medium before or has never had any visionary experiences can be disturbed by the realization that he or she is receiving communications from the spirits. When this happens, the receptor is inclined to disbelieve that his or her thoughts and feelings are actually coming from the spirits. But eventually he or she will begin to realize that these impressions are important to the session's topic or concerns. It is similar to realizing that you are holding a piece of a puzzle that the group is trying to put together. If this happens to you, you should express your thought or feeling to the group. In fact your impressions may become so strong and powerful that you feel you *cannot* resist expressing them. You can simply say, "I think I may be picking up something here." And then a good medium will help you say what you need to say.

A good medium will also be attentive to the ways that a particular session may focus around a sitter and not become envious or upset because the limelight has shifted away from the medium. Respect for the wishes of the spirits is paramount. When they indicate that they are working directly with a particular sitter, encourage that person to maintain the contact and dialogue with the spirit.

MESSAGES THROUGH A NEW MEDIUM

A group of sitters who had been meeting regularly with a medium named Stephen discovered one night that their spirit contact had special information he wanted to convey directly through one of the sitters. The group's purposes varied from session to session, but recently a spirit named Swort, who had died during the Black Plague in Europe in the fourteenth century, had been making regular appearances at their table. At his first visit two members of the group decided to question Swort about disease. One sitter's mother had cancer; the other had a good friend dying of AIDS. Since then the seance group had met as a kind of mini-seminar, with Swort answering their questions about illness, plague, and death.

On this particular night Jeffrey, a sitter who had not been as interested in these sessions with Swort as had the others, was surprised when the focus of the session turned toward him. The group had gathered as usual around the table with the lights off, a single candle burning in the center. They rested their hands on the table and closed their eyes. Stephen went into a light trance and invoked Swort, who presently showed up. The usual procedure was for members of the circle to ask the spirit questions that they had prepared in advance, but they had agreed that they need not stick rigidly to their list if the discussion went in other directions.

"Are we being punished for polluting the environment?" Peggy began when Swort was present.

"Disease always comes from the environment," answered Stephen, channeling Swort. "You cannot escape what you do to the earth around you."

"But are things like cancer, AIDS, and diabetes a result of how we live today?"

Swort answered, "Your diseases always reflect some truth about how you live."

The questions and answers continued like this for about ten minutes. Then Jeffrey said softly, "I think I'm hearing something from Swort that he wants me to tell you."

Stephen encouraged him. "Take your time and listen carefully before you speak." Jeffrey took a deep breath, and a slight smile appeared on his lips. Then he spoke in his normal voice.

"We need to slow down, go slow, or rest more—something like that."

Mary, another sitter, asked, "What do you mean?"

Jeffrey took another deep breath and waited a moment. "Says . . . says . . . the earth has a pace that we do not live by or respect. We go too fast."

Stephen then asked, "And is that why so many people get sick today?" Stephen posed a leading question because he knew Jeffrey was not used to channeling a spirit. From experience Stephen knew that often a sitter needs to be coaxed into letting the spirits speak freely.

"Says . . . yes, yes," replied Jeffrey, gaining more confidence. "Our bodies wear down because we push ourselves too much. The environment too. Says . . . it's a combination of things. Us. The earth. Pollution. In other times, too, people got sick from not living more carefully."

Stephen asked if anyone had other questions for Swort that they wanted to direct to Jeffrey. Many did, and the rest of the seance focused on Jeffrey's contact with the fourteenth-century spirit. After a while Jeffrey felt tired and was not sure he was hearing Swort. At that point he knew that either Swort had left or he no longer wanted to speak through Jeffrey. "I think that's all," he said to the group.

Stephen asked, "Swort, do you have more to tell us through anyone here tonight?" No reply. Stephen asked his own spirit guide, "Has Swort gone for the night?" The answer was yes.

POSITIONS AROUND THE TABLE

There are no hard and fast rules governing the way people are positioned around the table for a seance. Different mediums and circles have their preferences, and each group will have to work out its own best arrangements.

Some circles alternate men and women for the sake of gender balance. A table with all the men at one end and the women at the other seems lopsided to some mediums. But it isn't necessary to achieve an equal number of men and women. If your circle is composed of *all* men or all women, you won't have to concern yourself; just be sure to make good use of the individual personalities of the seance participants. You can base the mix or arrangement on the particular characteristics of individuals themselves, rather than on stereotyped assumptions about male and female energies. Place people so that you balance extroverts and introverts, talkers and nontalkers, active types and passive types, head people and heart people.

Most important are the two people selected to sit on either side of the medium. They should be warm and supportive people who radiate an openness and gentleness. Most mediums would rather have good-natured, heartfelt personalities next to them than colder, rational, intellectual types. For many mediums, seance work is heart work more than head work. The head can get in the way, raising objections, deceiving, criticizing, and disbelieving. The heart is less deceptive. Our hearts often know things that our heads have not made up their minds about. The energy from warm, openhearted men and women also makes spirits feel welcome and at ease.

You may want to arrange people according to their age or experience in seances. Place younger sitters and guests who have not attended many seances next to or between older members and those who know what to expect. This will make the less experienced feel more secure. Sometimes a nod or touch of the hand from a more experienced sitter can reassure a newcomer not to worry about what may or may not be occurring when spirit contact has been made. The mix and arrangement of sitters is a very individual issue. Experimentation is sometimes the only way to discover what works best for a particular circle. Don't hesitate, if spirits do not seem to be coming after several minutes, to ask people to change places. This should be done without making any moral judgment about those who are asked to move. In fact no reason has to be given. The medium or leader can simply suggest that Jack try changing places with Judy for a while to see if that helps. No one need be told that he or she is in the "wrong" place.

MEDIUM, HOST, RECORDER, AND LEADER

An ongoing circle that meets regularly will want to establish certain roles or offices among its members, although these can rotate so that the same person does not always have to perform the same tasks.

The medium, of course, plays the main role, but if your circle is a learning or study circle you might rotate this office as well. Let each person have a chance to be the "medium for the night" to develop his or her skills. If one person is more successful than the others, of course, he or she may emerge as the primary medium for your group.

It is not unusual for a group to have several mediums. You should decide, before sitting, which medium will begin the session, and all present should respect that medium's right to channel the spirits who come. Nevertheless, as we have seen, the spirits may make their own intentions known and elect to work with someone else. It is important for everyone present to allow the "chosen" medium to channel spirit communication if the spirits indicate that he or she should do so.

One member of the circle should host the sessions, and this need not be the medium. The host generally takes care of mundane preparations, such as shopping for snacks and beverages and cleaning the house.

A circle should also have a recorder who keeps a log of the sessions, noting which spirits came, what the communications were about, and in what ways the session was a success or failure. If you meet frequently, you will begin to gather too much information to retain in your memory. A member who misses a gathering can read the log before you meet again. Some spirits will return more than once, and it is helpful to have a record of what they said on previous occasions. After a session you can look up and compare the new information to that conveyed during previous visitations. If you intend to contact a specific spirit, you may want to review the questions you asked it at other seances and refresh your memory about the answers it gave. Sometimes months or years go by between visits by the same spirits, and it may be difficult to remember what they said and when they came.

The recorder may write down the communications as they occur if there is enough light in the room. Or the material can be recorded during the break immediately after a session.

Some circles tape-record sessions; others find that a tape recorder is not reliable, often malfunctioning when spirits are present. (This may be caused by the intense energy field in the room.) When the tape is replayed, you may hear nothing but static. Some mediums become self-conscious when they know they are being taped. Performance anxiety is not conducive to good work. On the other hand, a tape may pick up sounds or spirit voices that were not audible during the seance. Afterward, the tape may help sitters fill in gaps or clear up uncertainties in the message. Of course the extra sounds or voices on the tape may also be garbled or indistinct, and sitters may not agree on what they are hearing. You will have to experiment on your own to see whether you want to tape your sessions.

A circle should also have an official leader, who need not be the medium, recorder, or host. The leader usually facilitates the seance by arranging the date, time, and location of each sitting. It is generally he or she who formally calls the meeting together, suggesting when to break or end the seance. The leader might also offer the opening prayer or lead a meditation at the beginning of a seance to raise the group's energy and put the sitters into a contemplative, receptive attitude. This procedure will be explained more fully in Chapter 5.

THE DEVELOPMENT CIRCLE

The famous psychic and medium Eileen Garrett went through a period in her early life when she had visions and psychic occurrences that left her bewildered and upset. She saw unpleasant events before they happened; premonitions of future disasters broke through into her consciousness. She sensed the oncoming and early deaths of her two children who died of meningitis. She foresaw her second husband being killed in World War I. People and friends, including her first husband, whom she later divorced, encouraged her to stop having visions, as if she could turn them off and on like tap water. Like many people gifted with psychic abilities, Garrett was unsure of what to make of the "bizarre" events in her life. Should she try to stop the visions and premonitions as well-wishers suggested? Could her powers be used to make life more meaningful? Could they serve others? Were they potentially harmful to her psychological well-being and her ability to function in society?

To answer these questions, Garrett did what others have done: she read up on paranormal psychology, attended lectures on metaphysical subjects, and joined a spiritualist society. One of the great dangers for people who have spontaneous psychic experiences is that they will feel isolated from the rest of humanity and retreat into their own world of uncertainty and confusion. Participation in clubs or organizations of like-minded people can break the isolation, make the newly awakening medium feel more self-confident, and, most of all, help develop his or her psychic gifts.

In addition to her study of paranormal phenomena, Eileen Garrett began attending seances, where she discovered her mediumistic powers. On one occasion she fell spontaneously into a deep trance, during which the spirits of the deceased spoke through her. She continued to attend seances and also sought out the advice and counsel of a famous Swiss psychic. It was he who helped her meet her first spirit guide, Uvani.

Even famous mediums have required help in developing their gifts; many have found the seance circle a perfect place to begin. The development circle is a highly recommended method for discovering whether you have mediumship talents and, if you do, for learning to perfect them so they can serve both you and others. The development circle is a kind of school for mediums, a living laboratory to let your talents unfold. Development or learning circles are usually composed of either people who have just recently become aware of their ability to contact the dead or people who want to acquire these abilities.

Development circles can be run by students themselves or facilitated by a more experienced medium. Obviously, if the circle contains more experienced mediums who are willing to help the newer ones along, all will learn more quickly and a lot of time can be saved by not having to "reinvent the wheel." But if you don't know any mediums who are willing to teach you, don't hesitate to begin on your own. The real teaching comes from the spirits anyway, and if you approach the sessions intelligently and sensitively, you can make great progress.

(A development circle follows the same procedures as a regular seance, and these will be explained in more detail in the next chapter. The rest of this chapter contains guidelines for conducting development circles; these should be applied to the more complete directions in the next chapter.)

Not everyone in the development circle has to want to be a medium or have mediumistic talents. As in any circle, the presence of sitters is important to create the group energy field. A development circle can contain friends and sympathetic acquaintances who share and support your interests and who will encourage you and others in your evolution as mediums.

As mentioned earlier, the best number of sitters for a circle is somewhere between four or five and twelve or thirteen, although often two or three people can have remarkable results. Having more than twelve or thirteen people can be intimidating for most beginners. Performance anxiety is very detrimental, and the more people present, the larger the "audience" and thus the chance of not being able to relax and open up to your spirit guides.

Members should commit themselves, as much as possible, to attending regularly (frequency of meetings is discussed later in this chapter) so that the group has continuity. It also helps to meet in the same room and around the same table, since familiar visual and environmental cues facilitate the shifting of consciousness. Beginners find it easier to alter their consciousness in the presence of people and objects that they associate with this type of work.

As in other circles, sitters should avoid rivalry, competition, or one-upmanship, none of which are conducive to learning or feeling at ease. If the intention is for everyone or several beginners to learn mediumship skills, one person dominating the seance can deprive the others of the chance to progress. Someone "too psychic" can unwittingly obstruct the meeting, as we have seen. Development circles should not include skeptics, especially those who are hostile or suspicious. More experienced mediums can handle skeptical sitters (in fact, as mentioned previously, some mediums even encourage them to attend as a kind of mission to educate others about the spirit world), but learners should be surrounded by people whose energy is compatible with their own.

If after several sittings no one seems to be making any progress, you might consider changing the sitters. Ask those who have become discouraged to leave, and invite others. Sometimes changing the group is necessary to achieve the right mix. Similarly, the group's efforts should be directed to the person whose skills are unfolding at the moment. This may vary from session to session. The point is to encourage and support whomever the spirits contact.

As noted earlier, some mediums prefer that a circle have an equal number of men and women, and they try to achieve this balance. In recent years, however, especially with the rise of separate women's and men's movements, we have learned that spiritual work can progress very rapidly and deeply when people work in groups that are all male or all female. Decide this issue among yourselves and do whatever seems right for your group. While both mixed circles and one-gender circles can function very well, it's possible that a "wrong" mix or an unbalanced ratio could work against a particular group of people. You can find out only through trial and error.

If your group seems to be making no progress whatsoever, you might consider hiring a professional medium to join you for a few sessions or asking someone whose mediumship skills are more highly developed to help out. Often this "jump-starting" brings dramatic results, and after a few sessions you can continue on your own. See the Appendix for suggestions on how to find a medium.

What to Expect in a Development Circle

Procedures for a development circle are similar to those for running any seance, but the intention here is focused specifically on creating and strengthening the group's connections with the spirit world *in general*. For this reason you should not try to contact a specific spirit or try to test the spirits too early to establish their identities or truthfulness. This is not to say that you should deal uncritically with the spirits who manifest, but attempting to learn too many details and specific information can lead to confusing and contradictory answers that undermine your confidence. The first major step in becoming a medium is to acquire self-confidence in your ability to tap into the stream of dialogue between the worlds of the living and the deceased. Asking the spirits for overly specific and minutely detailed information about themselves or other issues can come later.

So, for example, if a spirit tells you that he lived in the

last century, accept that. If you then ask for a specific year and he doesn't answer, let it go. Let the spirit offer the details and the information that is important to him or her. Avoid asking questions just to satisfy your own curiosity. Most seances end without providing all the information you wanted to know anyway, and learning how to accept that is part of your training. Sometimes what we think is important to know in the early stages of a seance turns out not to be all that significant. It is better, especially while you are still a beginner, to let the spirits direct the dialogue. So, if a spirit does not answer a specific question, drop it. What is important at this stage is the contact you have made, not the amount of information you can gather.

An effective approach is to acknowledge the spirits that come and to ask them what their intention is and what they want to talk about. Put your own interests and curiosities on the back burner for a while and concentrate on being cooperative and expressing goodwill. A confrontational or distrusting attitude will repel higher spirits and may attract less desirable spirits, who feed on your negativity. Remember, your initial goal in development circles is to create and strengthen your natural connections with the otherworld, to discover the channels for letting spirit communications flow freely, and to build a community of people that includes both the living and the dead.

As you sit patiently waiting for a sign that a spirit is present, pay attention to the flow of thoughts and feelings passing through you. Keep in mind that the spirits "plug into" our mental and emotional energy, the group's thoughts and feelings at the present moment. When a word, image, thought, feeling, or idea seems to be making a strong impression on you, as if it were tugging at you to get your attention, honor it and let it unfold. When the moment seems right, tell it to the group so that it becomes part of their consciousness. For example, you might say "I am getting the impression of a young woman" or "I'm getting the strong feeling of sorrow." Sit quietly for a while with that impression. When the idea or image becomes stronger or clearer or begins to shift into a more complex impression or statement, speak again. Anyone in the circle who experiences this evolution and development of the image can voice it. Go slowly, because the spirit may be using more than one of you to initiate the dialogue. Spirits sometimes "try out" different sitters to see who is the most compatible, and the initial communication arises piecemeal from several sitters.

At some point one sitter may feel that the spirit is focused primarily on her or him. When this happens, the group should sit back and let the sitter carry on the dialogue. Or other sitters can support the contact by asking the spirit questions through the sitter, slowly, carefully, and openheartedly, avoiding all sense of distrust or suspicion.

In these early stages of development and in the early stages of any session when contact has just been made, avoid analyzing what the spirits say. This is not always easy to do. The rational side of our minds cannot easily tune itself down and accept experiences on their own terms. It is natural for us to want to pick at ideas and take them apart, looking for reasons and explanations for things. This can frustrate higher spirits.

Sometimes spirits communicate very rapidly. A spirit may go from step A to step C, sidestepping B altogether, and then go from C to G! Many of us need the methodical procedure of taking one step at a time because we feel uneasy about jumping ahead or (to use a phrase fraught with dire warning) "jumping to conclusions." And yet we all have moments of intuitive insight when we are inspired by an idea that comes out of the blue. Speaking with spirits often resembles this kind of spontaneous knowing and understanding, more than the rational, linear thinking that we may be more comfortable with. Training to be a better medium means learning to trust the mystical and nonrational faculties of your psyche so that you receive information and knowledge in a manner similar to the way spirits communicate. So be prepared for flashes of insight as well as the deep understanding that grows slowly and unfolds in its own good time.

Finding Sitters for a Development Circle

It takes only two people to begin a development circle, but sometimes finding that second person can be a challenge. If you have a friend who shares your interest in spirit communication, you can simply ask him or her to study with you, read up on spiritualism, and apply the techniques and procedures in this book. With some luck, you'll each find one more person, and the circle will start to grow. Begin by meeting at least once a week, but two or even three times a week would be more helpful, especially at first.

If you know of no one you can ask directly, here are some approaches you might take:

• Call a local branch of the Unitarian-Universalist Church or Unitarian Fellowship and ask the pastor if any of the members are interested in spiritualism or hold spiritualist meetings. People in the Unitarian-Universalist Church are, as a rule, very open-minded and inquisitive about alternative approaches to spirituality. It is not uncommon to find a strong interest in metaphysical subjects among its members.

• Ask the manager of a local bookstore, especially one that carries books on metaphysical and spiritualist topics, if he or she knows any regular customers who are interested in the subject. Often the manager of a used, specialty, or rare bookstore knows the customers' individual interests, since customers frequently ask the manager to watch for books on certain subjects.

• Post notices on local bulletin boards in your community stating that you are interested in beginning a "study group" to read about and discuss issues related to "death and the afterlife." When people phone or contact you, ask what their specific interests are. By taking this approach, rather than just advertising that you are beginning a seance group, you will avoid getting crank calls and you can screen out undesirable people. Most likely the average person will not be familiar with the phrase *development circle* anyway. However, if you live in a free-thinking community, you might just announce that you are hoping to create a group of people to study and practice mediumistic skills. Bulletin boards likely to be read by prospective sitters can be found at health and natural food stores, in metaphysical bookstores, or college campuses, and in Unitarian-Universalist churches.

• Check your local alternative or "New Age" newspaper or magazine covering issues related to health, the metaphysical, and spiritual topics. You might find personal ads from readers who already hold seances or who are hoping to meet others with whom they can start a circle. If not, you could place an ad yourself, either openly or along the guidelines suggested for posting up notices on bulletin boards.

• Watch for ads targeted to people who want to begin or join groups that study related topics, such as dreams, parapsychology, shamanism, metaphysics, and alternative spiritual practices. Call the contact person and see if his or her interests include seance work.

When word gets around that you hold seances (and it will), do not be surprised if friends, acquaintances, even strangers begin to call, asking if they can join you. Use the guidelines in this chapter to make decisions about whom you will let sit in your circles, keeping in mind that there are no passive observers in a seance circle. Everyone who sits with you plays an active, responsible role.

ॐ 5 ॐ

HOLDING A SEANCE

A SUMMER AGO MY BROTHER-IN-LAW ERIC AND I
planned to remember the second anniversary of my sister's
death by spending some time reminiscing about her and
sharing with each other how her leaving us has changed
our lives. We decided to hike out on a bluff that overhangs
the Hudson River in New York State to be alone for the
afternoon and to think and talk about Gail. It was a cloudy,
warm, blustery day, and even though it was the height of
summer, there was an eerie emptiness on the river, which
is usually teeming with sailboats, skiers, and windsurfers.
The river was actually deserted. A light mist fell off and on.

As we sat alone and talked about Gail, we noticed a
large, attentive hawk circling around us, at first a few feet
over our heads and then just a slight distance below us
from where we sat on the edge of the bluff. It is not
unusual to see hawks along the river, but this one came
exceptionally and startlingly close. We felt as if we could
have touched her had she circled in just a few feet closer.
When the mist threatened to turn to heavier rain, we

decided to leave, and as we descended the rocky trail from the top of the bluff, we saw three deer walking calmly toward us, just a few yards off the path. We froze in our tracks, hoping the deer would not dash off as deer usually do when they sense the presence of humans, but these deer clearly were not frightened. They walked right up, looked over at us, staying a few feet to the side, and then passed slowly by.

I said to Eric, who is from Ohio, "I've been coming to this spot on the river at least once a month in every season for the last five years, and I have never seen deer or deer signs out here." The narrow spit of land we were on sticks out into the Hudson and is cut off from thousands of acres of wildlife by a major road and two railroad tracks. Why would deer risk being hit by cars and trains when they had more than enough forested mountain slopes on the other side of the road and rails? Then Eric explained it. "Hawk and deer," he said. "These are Gail's animal spirits."

My sister and her husband valued the natural world and the role that the spirits of nature play in our lives. As they studied Native American traditions and the earth-centered spiritualities in other cultures, they learned to recognize the helping animal spirits that enrich our lives. Hawk and deer. They were Gail's spirit helpers while she was alive, and they seemed to be her messengers to us after her death. I have not seen deer out on that point of land since that summer's day.

Was sitting high above the Hudson River that afternoon a seance? In a way it was, although it had not been our intention to contact Gail or the animal spirits that were her guides. This was a spontaneous seance, an unexpected flow of communication between the worlds of the living and the dead. It was just one incident among many in which our loved ones who have passed on continue to make their presence known in our lives. When Eric and I returned to the car (and heard on the radio that there were tornado warnings out for the Hudson Valley—*that's* why no boats were on the river!), we felt as certain that we had spent time with Gail as we would have had we held a formal seance and intentionally invited her spirit to join us and speak to us.

There is more than one way to hold a seance. In this chapter we will look at the practical steps you can use to prepare for and begin a formal seance. Each circle of sitters will decide for itself the preparations and rituals that best create the atmosphere for conducting a seance. There are virtually no right or wrong ways to do it, except as you discover from your own experience. The following guidelines are merely suggestions to get you started. As you continue to sit together on succeeding occasions, you will most likely want to adapt these guidelines, discarding some altogether and modifying others as you develop your own procedures.

PREPARING THE ROOM

Make the room as comfortable as possible. The spirits, of course, don't really care if the room is cluttered or messy, but humans often do. A clean, tidy, inviting area is more conducive to reflective work than a dirty, cramped area where people have trouble relaxing and getting comfortable.

Set up a table and chairs. Some groups always use the same table, such as a dining table or a card table. The chairs should be comfortable but straight enough so that it is not awkward to sit attentively at the table. Soft, overstuffed easy chairs are not a good idea since they are hard to pull up to a table and they tend to put people to sleep.

The question of lighting is debated among mediums and sitters. Some groups work in total darkness, turning off all the lights and drawing the curtains. Others turn off the lights but allow the natural light from outside to come in. Some seances are held by candlelight. Most people want to dim the lighting in some way for several reasons.

First, a dimly lit room is conducive to shifting consciousness and going into trance. Anytime you create a dimmer lighting arrangement for a room (even if you don't plan on doing any type of visionary work), you instinctively sense a nonordinary, otherworldly atmosphere. Another practical reason for a dimly lit or dark room is so that the sitters do not distract each other or become distracted by the furnishings in the room.

Darkness may also help some spirits communicate. It has been suggested that recently departed spirits may feel self-conscious and not want to be seen. We may never know while we are alive just how spirits manifest themselves so they can be seen physically, but the spirits themselves report that apparitions are tricky and require extra energy and the right conditions. A recently departed spirit who is not sure of the laws governing apparitions may be more comfortable in a darkened room. It is also possible that some spirits under certain conditions cannot control their apparitions. A self-conscious or inexperienced spirit may feel more secure when visibility in the room is reduced.

Many sitters like to keep their eyes closed during a seance, but this is not necessary. There are moments in a seance when you may need to open your eyes. A candle at the center of the table can act as a focal point to fix your attention on. Do not, however, place a candle on the table if you know that the spirits communicate with you through table tipping. A writing or speaking medium does not need to worry about a candle sliding off the table. But even so, if a spirit who wants to tip the table comes, the candle must be removed quickly at the first indication that the table is getting active.

Other practical preparations include turning off the phone, stopping clocks that tick or chime, putting pets outside. Once I attended a seance in a room that had a wind chime just outside the window. Even though it was winter and the window was closed tightly, a strong wind blew up during the evening's work, and the wind chime tinkled nonstop. We had taped the evening's session, and afterward we eagerly played back the tape because several sitters, including me, had heard noises, footsteps, and voices during the course of the sitting. Fortunately the tape had picked up our dialogue, so we had a good record of what was said, but when we listened closely for the extra spirit sounds, all we could hear was the wind chime.

BEGINNING THE SEANCE

Sit with your hands resting lightly on the tabletop. Some groups space their hands and spread their fingers so that their little fingers touch. This reinforces the sense of oneness and creates an unbroken circle of contact and a sense of community and purpose. You do not need to hold this position throughout the seance, but just until the spirits arrive. Feet should be flat on the floor and backs erect. In general each sitter should try to maintain an alert and upright position during the seance, but comfort should win out over unnaturally stiff or rigid positions. A leg going to sleep or an aching back is distracting and adds nothing to the state of consciousness needed to discern spirits.

Most groups use some form of meditative or relaxation techniques either before they sit down at the table or

THE BRIDGE

Janice and her circle use the table-tipping method for spirit communication. They sit in a darkened room around a card table, and each member places his or her hands lightly on the table. Janice goes into a trance, calls her spirit contact, and asks if there are any spirits who want to make contact. Janice and her group believe that because they have been meeting for so long, they are well known in the spirit world and spirits routinely come to their sessions for many different reasons. Her circle is also respected in the town where they live and is called on now and then for local hauntings, police work, and people grieving over the deaths of loved ones.

One night, when the group had gathered, the table tipped twice for yes when Janice asked if anyone was there. "Have we spoken with you before?" she asked. One tip: no. "What is your name?"

At this question, Mark, sitting on Janice's right, said "A," then Shana next to him said "B," and they proceeded around the table, each person stating the next letter of the alphabet. No table tips occurred until they got to N, when the table tipped twice. Yes. (When going through the alphabet, it is not necessary for spirits to indicate the wrong letters, just the correct ones.) Then, since the next letter was probably a vowel, they ran through the vowels, beginning with A. At O the table tipped twice. The group then learned that the next letter was N. Eventually the spirit spelled out NO NAME.

"So you will not tell us your name?" Janice questioned the spirit. Two tips. "Do you have a message for us?" Two more tips—big tips that lifted the end of the table farther off the floor than it had been rising.

The group then began spelling out words. The first word was BRIDGE. They began on the next word and received the letters C-O-L-L-A. *Immediately Brian, who was quick to complete words before all the letters arrived, guessed* COLLAPSE.

The table lifted twice and rather violently.

"A bridge is going to collapse?!" another member exclaimed.

At this question the table began bouncing up and down as if in a fit of excitement.

Then the group asked, "Where?"

And No Name spelled out the answer "In town."

Janice asked the spirit to be more specific since there were several bridges in town, but the table refused to budge. The group sat in awed silence, wondering why No Name remained silent or had left. One of them suggested it was a prankster spirit just having some fun with them. But Mark thought differently.

"I think we should take the message seriously," he advised the group. "Maybe this is a warning about a bridge that is going to collapse. We should notify the highway department tomorrow."

The next day Janice phoned the highway commissioner and told him what had occurred at the seance. Because the seance group had a good reputation in the community, the commissioner took the warning seriously. Work crews inspected the local bridges over the next week. They discovered that one of the older bridges had a very defective support beam that was in serious need of repair. Workers mended it, and the bridge did not collapse.

immediately upon taking their seats. These vary from group to group. The common goal, however, is to relax and acquire a shifted state of awareness. Deep breathing works well for most people. A few moments of slow, rhythmic breathing with eyes closed not only relax us but create a sense of group spirit. Breathing is a sacred act in many spiritual traditions and an important element in some meditation practices. Breathing was our first act after birth, and one of our breaths will be our last act before we pass on into the next world. Conscious breathing, therefore, is a natural ceremonial activity before a seance.

Other methods for relaxing and altering awareness include chanting a certain sound that your group decides on (such as om), visualizing a selected color (many people associate blue with the soul), or even counting slowly in unison from one to ten or twenty or from twenty down to one.

Some groups use energy-raising techniques. One method to raise energy is to hold hands and feel the energy moving from the person on your right, up your arm, across your chest, and down your left arm into the hand of the person on your left. Visualize the flow of energy circling through the group, picking up speed as it makes the rounds. You can do this exercise silently, or a leader might talk the group through the process, especially if it is new to some.

Most groups begin with a prayer or two. This need not be more than one or two sentences, and it can be directed to the Divine Spirit and/or the group's contacts and helping spirits. A group that meets regularly can decide what terms to use in referring to the Divine Spirit. If your sitters come from a mixture of religious backgrounds, you may have to discuss the options and vote on an appellation that everyone can agree to use. God, Goddess, Lord, Lady, Creator, Divine Spirit, Great Spirit, Jesus, Mary, the Gods/ Goddesses, All-That-Is, the One-Who-Is, the Universal Power: choose a name that all are comfortable using. Here are some sample prayers and invocations:

"We ask that the Divine Spirit and all our Guides and Guardians be present and watch over our work tonight."

"May the Gods and Spirits of the Universe guide us this evening."

"We pray that the Universal Power and all our Spirit Companions put us in contact with good and helpful spirits and protect us from mischief and harm from troubled spirits."

"May the Powers of the Cosmos that protect and guard us bless us and the spirits who join us tonight."

The prayer can remain the same from week to week and be offered by the leader or the same sitter; or you can rotate this office and let each person create his or her own invocation, using the terms and sentiments that the group has agreed on as being expressive of its beliefs.

MAKING CONTACT

When the group is relaxed and the opening prayer has been said, sit in silence for a few moments. During this time the medium should do what he or she needs to do to go into trance or contact his or her spirit guide. The leader should watch closely and inform the group that the medium "is under" or is "ready." (In a developed circle or with a new medium, it may take a few sessions before the leader knows when the medium is in trance.) If the me-

dium does not need to induce a deeper state of consciousness than the rest of the group, you should still pause for a
few moments as everyone lets his or her consciousness
expand and open to the surrounding vibrations and energies.

When this has been done, the leader or medium then
begins in one of two ways, depending on the purpose for
the seance: to contact a specific spirit or to allow a spirit to
contact the group.

If you plan to contact a specific spirit, the medium
then calls that spirit by name or asks his or her guide to
fetch that spirit by name. Stating the complete name of the
spirit is important. There is an infinity of spirits in the
universe. It is important that you summon the correct one
and that your spirit guide know specifically whom you are
inviting to your seance. Say, "We would like to make
contact with James Robert Jones." It also helps to give the
reason for the contact. For example, inform the spirit that
a relative or close friend wants to speak with him. Say
something like "Your brother is here tonight and wishes to
speak with you."

Some mediums make it a practice never to call a
specific spirit directly for fear that, hearing the call, the
spirit may interrupt other more important matters to join
the seance, thinking there is a crisis or an emergency
involving former friends or family members. I know one
medium who always asks her spirit guide to find out if a
desired spirit can come. Sometimes she asks for "anyone
who knows about the desired spirit" to come and tell the
circle whether the spirit is available. If it is permissible for
the spirit to come, the medium then asks the go-between to
fetch the spirit. I admire this medium's concern for not
wanting to divert a spirit from its current path unnecessar-
ily. Such consideration for the spirits' welfare should be a

hallmark of all mediums. But there is considerable evidence from countless seances that this is not a prevalent problem because the more highly evolved spirits can do several things at once, and if a lower spirit cannot or should not interrupt its current work or mission, it will most likely not do so.

If you are not invoking a particular spirit, ask, "Are there any spirits present?" Continue to sit silently and wait for a response. If there is no response within a minute or two, ask the question again. If there is still no response, ask, "Do we need to make any changes in the room or at the table?" In other words, should the room be darker (or brighter)? Should the arrangement of sitters around the table be changed?

In many cases the medium will begin at this point to receive messages visually, aurally, or intuitively, which other sitters may or may not be aware of, and will transmit the information to all present. If, on the other hand, the table moves or raps are heard after you ask this question, the leader or medium should tell the spirits the code that the group uses—for example, one rap or tip for no, two raps or tips for yes—then ask what needs to be done in short, unambiguous, one-part questions, such as "Should we turn off all the lights?" or "Should we change seats?"

If the answer to this question is yes, ask if the person to the right of the medium should move, then wait for an answer. Then proceed around the table, asking who should move and be seated next to whom. When you finally have the positioning that pleases the spirits, you can begin to ask the following questions to establish a better contact.

If you have invoked a particular spirit, ask, "Are you James Robert Jones?" If you have asked simply whether there are any spirits present, ask "Have you been here before?" or "Have we spoken with you before?" It is always good to establish early whether the spirit who is with you is an "old friend" or someone new. If it has been present on other occasions, you can get right down to business. If it is a spirit new to your group, ask the following standard introductory questions.

"What is your name?" If the medium is channeling information verbally, she or he will now speak the spirit's name. If the table is tipping, begin with the letter A and proceed around the table, each sitter saying the next letter of the alphabet until the table tips twice (meaning yes). Then begin again with B and go around until you get the next letter. When you suspect that the upcoming letter is a vowel, run through the vowels rather than the entire alphabet. Table tipping is time consuming, but you will eventually grow accustomed to the pacing. Use primarily yes-or-no questions until you need a specific word or name, then change to the alphabet.

The spirit may not give you its name at this point. That may come later. (See the next chapter on ways to verify a spirit's identity and how to handle impostors.)

Other information that is important to know early in the contact is whether the spirit is in trouble or pain and wants the circle to help alleviate it. You can ask, "Are you troubled or worried?" Then find out the cause and specifically ask what the group or some members of the group can do to help.

Then go on to the next series of questions concerning the spirit's intentions. "Do you have a message for us?" "Is it for someone in particular?" "Is it for someone at the table?" "Is it for someone who is not here tonight?" If yes, then ask for whom it is intended. Once you have determined that the spirit has a message and you learn whom it is for, go on to find out what it is about.

If the medium is speaking or writing, he or she can

deliver the message. If the table is tipping, begin by asking "What is the message about?" rather than "What is the message?" With this approach the spirit can begin by spelling out the key words of the message. As the content of the message becomes clearer, you can begin to ask questions that anticipate the meaning. For example, if the first word spelled is *health,* and you know that the message is for Adrian at the table, your next question might be "Is Adrian's health in danger?" The next inquiry might be "What part of his body is affected?" And so forth.

This is the standard procedure for getting from a spirit information intended for a specific person or for the group as a whole. The message might be general information about the condition of the world or a request that the group or someone in the group perform some service for the spirit. A channeling medium might simply deliver a lengthy communication from a spirit or spirits, in the form of either a monologue or an essay, or the information may come in the form of a dialogue between the medium and the spirit or between sitters and the medium speaking for the spirit. Sometimes channeled communications need to be drawn out by specific questions. When good contact has been made, the leader of the circle should begin asking the usual set of questions to get the dialogue going. At some point when it seems appropriate or when the spirit indicates it wants to speak to specific sitters, the other sitters ease their way into the conversation, asking questions and responding to questions from the spirit.

A writing medium should have plenty of sheets of paper available before the seance begins. Writing often comes quickly and profusely, using up page after page. Also, sometimes the leader will take the page after an answer has been written or when the medium pauses and read it to the group. Then another question can be asked, and the medium has a fresh sheet of paper to write on.

As mentioned in the previous chapter, when sitters feel that the spirits are communicating directly to them, by-passing the medium, they should share the impressions or messages they receive with the rest of the circle.

The Ouija Board

You may want to consider using a Ouija board, which has been a mainstay in many people's understanding and practice of mediumship for several generations, when you first begin holding seances. Although it has the reputation of being something of a parlor game since its introduction by a famous board game company in the early part of this century, it can be a useful tool for seances. The famous medium Jane Roberts, who channeled several volumes of valuable information from a spirit named Seth, first encountered him on a Ouija board. Seth gave Roberts information by writing it out on the board. Eventually Roberts's mind began picking up the messages faster than the planchette could spell out the words, so she dispensed with the Ouija board and began direct channeling. Her husband taped the sessions, transcribed them later, and eventually published them as *Seth Speaks*, the first in a series of Seth books.

If you decide to use a Ouija board in your seance work, be sure to grant the board the same respect as you do the rest of the proceedings. Some people report that playful or pesky spirits favor situations in which Ouija board users fail to treat the board with the seriousness it merits; remember that the board is not a toy. Also, if you have a board that has previously been used as a game, you might consider purchasing a new board for seance use only.

Instructions come with each board, but the principle and practice are rather simple. Sit across from your partner with the board resting on your knees. Place the planchette, or little table, on the board and lightly rest the tips of your fingers on its surface, your fingers on one side, your partner's on the other. The planchette moves across the board—which contains the letters of the alphabet, numbers from zero to nine, and the words *yes* and *no*—in response to questions.

Begin a seance with the Ouija board as you would any other seance, by preparing the room, spending a few moments relaxing, and creating a meditative state within yourselves. Then call the spirits. The point is not to just grab the board, dust it off, and begin. If you treat the Ouija board as a game or an idle pastime, you will not get very good results. The secret of a successful seance is not in the physical tools or setting but in the minds and hearts of the medium and sitters.

Ask questions that lend themselves to yes-or-no answers or can be spelled out rather simply. As the planchette moves across the board, it will come to rest on a letter, then proceed to move some more, coming to another letter as it spells out words. Yes and no answers are indicated by the planchette moving to those words in the corners of the board.

Saying Good-Bye and Taking a Break

At some point the spirit may announce that it has no more to say at this time and is leaving. If so, the medium and the sitters should express their thanks for the visit and say farewell. Or, rather than formally announcing that the session is over, the spirit might simply seem to be "fading." The communications are slower, the pauses grow longer, and the medium begins to feel that the "reception" is getting bad. When this happens, tell the spirit that the group is going to take a break and that you'll begin another session a bit later in case the spirit has more to say.

Some mediums can tell it is time to end a session by the fact that they get tired. This may also have some bearing on the fact that the spirits seem to fade or the communications become slower, less clear, or hard to receive. If you feel a considerable loss of energy occurring, take it as a sign that it's time to close. Prolonging a seance after you feel a drop in energy or when it becomes significantly difficult to maintain meaningful contact with a spirit is not wise because you may misread information or not present it clearly and accurately.

Some groups take a real break, with snacks and beverages, because visionary work can stimulate an appetite (it is not at all unusual to be ravenously hungry and thirsty after a few hours of seance work). Some groups go out for a snack afterward. Some snack between sessions. You'll discover how the members of your circle want to handle this. It is a good idea to have soft drinks, tea, or coffee handy even if you decide that your breaks will just be quiet moments without any eating or chatting.

The question of how "solemn" to be during a break, or even before and after the seance for that matter, will be decided by your circle or its leaders. The spirits don't require that we act as if we are in church! Many of them are fun-loving, give humorous answers, and seem to have fun at seances. So should you. On the other hand, your group must always be ready for the appearance of a grieving, lonely, or sorrowful spirit, so the group should agree that joking will stop when the seance gets serious.

During the break the recorder should enter a summary of the spirit conversation in the log. You may want to have it read just before you begin the next session, even

though only ten or fifteen minutes have gone by. It helps to
refresh everyone's memory.

PUBLIC AND PRIVATE SEANCES

If your group is made up primarily of beginners, you
probably should not hold public seances, that is, sittings
that are open to outsiders. Certainly you would not want to
advertise that you hold sittings and allow strangers to join
you if no one in the group knows who they are. It's best to
keep your circle small, homogeneous, and consistent. You
will find that you get better results from the same people
meeting regularly.

Spirits also get used to the same group and feel safe
and comfortable with it. Since spirits make use of the
group's energy, it is critical to know who is sitting in the
circle. Strangers may frighten some spirits off. And because
an unknown sitter at a seance is truly an "unknown quan-
tity," you run the risk of uncooperative energies, even
hostility or other obstructionary vibes. The wrong element
in a circle may alter the group aura so that the spirits you
want to contact cannot use it.

There is also the risk of a public seance taking on a
carnival atmosphere. Some people come simply out of
curiosity, hoping to be entertained, looking for bizarre
experiences to regale their friends with. These are not the
kinds of people you want in your circle. A seance is not a
stage act; it is a spiritual event.

Of course this does not mean that you can never have
a guest, someone who asks to come for some legitimate
reason. After all, if you conduct successful seances, you
have a responsibility to serve others, in both this world and
the next. Your circle may be the vehicle that will unite a

departed loved one with a family member or a close friend. You shouldn't hang a "Closed" or "Keep Out" sign over your door and bar all newcomers. But it is important that you know something about the person before the seance. Talk to him or her over the phone: ask prospective sitters why they want to attend, what their intentions are, what they are looking for.

Depending on how democratically you run your circles, you may want to report this information to the others in the group and vote on whether to let a prospective "client" join you. You should also decide whether that "client's" intention will be the only work of the evening or whether you will contact other spirits too and whether that guest can stay on for the other sittings that evening. Use your best judgment on these matters, keeping in mind that there are no unbendable rules regarding how you should conduct your sittings.

HAUNTINGS

A special type of seance is the one conducted to contact a spirit who is haunting a particular place. These sittings take place on the premises of the haunting, so they are run a little differently from weekly or monthly seances in your living room. But before we look at ways to hold a seance in a haunted house, let's take a look at the idea of hauntings and the types of spirits you may encounter at haunted places.

Why Spirits Stay

It is an ancient and universal belief that some places are haunted. Over the centuries a great deal of speculation has been offered as to why certain spirits haunt particular places and why some places appear to be haunted. The two are not always the same.

For example, many places have been strongly imprinted by the intense emotional events that took place there. Often these are of a tragic or violent nature, such as murders, suicides, battles, or rapes. Every human action energized by strong emotions leaves an imprint, like a photographic impression on film. Dowsers can pick up these emotions easily, even discovering the nature of the event. Most of us just get an eerie feeling in such places without knowing exactly what transpired there. General Patton, for instance, always knew when he was walking across an old battlefield. He could "feel" the energy of the fighting centuries after it occurred. Places that were formerly the sites of gallows or "hanging trees" can still make us shiver when we are near them.

This "field theory" of imprinted events applies to positive, joyful, happy occasions also, especially if a place was used regularly for joyous purposes. An old meadow or ceremonial site where peasant folk have performed the old religious rituals for centuries may still hold the aura of a sacred site, and we feel our blood stir with a sense of awe and reverence when we enter such a place. Sacred wells, old churches, and standing stones are prime examples of this type of imprinted energy.

An acquaintance of mine recalls the time she rented an apartment in an old Victorian house in Chicago while she was majoring in theater at school. After living there for a few months she got the distinct impression when she was in the room she used as a study that it had been a sewing room even though that is not how she used it. Later, after she had moved and was living somewhere else, she came across a current issue of a magazine on Chicago history. It attracted her attention because the cover depicted fancy theatrical costumes. The article inside was about a woman who had been a famous seamstress for the performing arts in Chicago and had sewn many costumes that had been worn on Chicago stages. And yes, the woman had been the former owner of the house my friend had rented while she was in school.

Places such as this are not, strictly speaking, "haunted," even though we sense the personality or character of the people who have imprinted their experiences there. In fact the person who left a dramatic imprint on a place may not even be dead. You might come upon a cliff, for example, and get one of those weird urges to jump off and commit suicide. You might be right in suspecting that perhaps this is where a famous suicide took place or that it is a "lover's leap" where many suicides occurred. But it is equally possible that only an hour before you arrived, a man may have contemplated suicide there, put up a tremendous struggle with himself, and decided he would not do it and went home. He's not dead, there's no ghost or spirit, and the place is obviously not haunted. The man simply imprinted his trauma on the field of energy present there. So be careful not to jump to conclusions about places that are charged with strong emotion.

Every place has spirits, or at least every place has spirits passing through, because spirits are not localized beings. They are literally everywhere. Most often these spirits are too "thin" or frivolous or transitory to be felt. The spirits who *haunt*, however, do manifest in an unusually localized and dramatic manner, having some particular attachment to a specific house or area. Unlike spirits who just pass through without being detected (or not detected very strongly), these spirits not only make their presence known but often *want* to make their presence known. Why do they haunt?

There are various explanations. Some mediums have suggested that only lower spirits who have not completely broken from their earthly life hang around their old places; these mediums seem to think that some less evolved spirits cannot break their attachment to a place but would be better off if they could.

But some mediums have met very evolved spirits who continue to hold a strong affection for a particular place, usually a place that played an important role in their spiritual evolution while alive and that continues to be a source of energy or inspiration for them in the spirit realm. For these reasons the spirit returns. Usually this higher spirit does not haunt the place constantly, as would spirits who cannot really break the attachment.

Often the higher spirit will be present at the site only on certain occasions or at certain times of year. There are places, for example, that are haunted only on a particular day of the year, when the spirit "returns." It may be the anniversary of some important event that occurred there in the spirit's mortal life, perhaps its death. A spirit may also appear at a certain place at each new or full moon because its mission is to be a "spirit of place" or a "ceremonial spirit" for mortals who worship or conduct rituals there.

An example of these "occasional spirits" are the Roman lemures, or wandering spirits of the dead. In ancient Rome three days in the middle of May were set aside each year as the Lemuria festival. During this time the wandering spirits visited their former homes, and family members were expected to acknowledge their presence and honor them.

There are many reasons why a spirit might hang around a particular place. A deceased person who has committed a serious crime may be required to remain at the scene of the crime as a kind of punishment for its deed. The victims of a crime may hang around also, looking for revenge or retribution. Some spirits haunt a place to protect the humans who live or work there. We may never be able to find out just why a particular spirit haunts a particular place.

The story is told of a man who in the 1960s rented a house just outside New York City that had once been owned by Washington Irving. When the man moved in, his dogs would not go into the house and his children could not sleep well at night. They felt chills and "saw" things that frightened them. Through the help of a psychic and some historical research, they discovered that there had once been a cottage on the property; two guests who had been invited to sleep there one night were found the next day hanging from the rafters. Apparently no one ever found out whether they had committed suicide or had been murdered, but local tradition said that the spirits of the two men had haunted the cottage. The psychic determined that when the cottage was torn down, the ghosts had moved into the main house. The psychic conducted a ritual to appease the ghosts, and from then on they stayed on the first floor of the house, without doing any harm. The dogs and the children were no longer upset. The ghosts always announced their presence, however, by chilling the air, making rattling noises, or flickering the lights for a moment or two.

Do spirits have a special attraction or affection for graveyards and old, deserted, or isolated ruins? Most mediums say no. Nevertheless, the dead do not lose their personalities completely when they pass to the other side. If a person enjoyed deserted isolated places while alive, it stands to reason that he or she might continue to do so after death. But most spirits seem to want or need, or just enjoy, human contact, so it is not likely that you will meet many spirits at deserted, spooky places that tend to drive people away. However, since spirits need our energy, to some extent, to make contact, a certain type of spirit might haunt gloomy swamps and graveyards because the kind of person who goes there to meet spirits has the type of energy the spirit wants. A trickster, for example, will play on the superstitions and fears of people and use their own frightened energy to make contact with them. The spirits who haunt graveyards and deserted houses may be just prankster spirits who get a kick out of scaring people who come there to be scared.

It is well known that one of the most effective methods for getting rid of a spirit who frightens you is to summon up your courage and defy the spirit's power over you. Without your fearful energy to draw on, the spirit is harmless. For example, if you wake up in the night in a strange hotel room or inn and feel the hands of a ghost around your neck, you may in fact have bruises there in the morning. Your fear was the energy that allowed the spirit to become dense enough to actually inflict pain on your body. If you did not succumb to the fear, you would most likely not have the strangulation marks on your neck the next day. In other words your belief and fear and your expectation that the ghost could harm you *allow* it to harm you. If you can learn to treat frightening spirits more casually and appear more powerful than they are, they will have no power over you. People who have had experiences with spirits who try to do physical harm claim that it helps to speak forcefully and tell them to leave.

It is possible that the grave of someone who is well loved and well remembered by the living may attract its spirit on occasion. If the family or friends visit the grave regularly, put flowers on it, keep it well trimmed and neat, the grave site could become a place where the spirit would attempt to contact the living if it needed to for some reason. Rituals of remembrance, regardless of where they take place, can have a luring effect on the deceased. Some cultures have a national "Day of the Dead" similar to our Memorial Day, All Souls' Day, and November Eve (now celebrated as Halloween, a day when the dead and the living traditionally visit "between the worlds"). Spirits are more "afoot" on these days because they respond to our efforts to commemorate their lives and honor their memories.

Haunted Houses

A fire department invited a local seance group to get rid of a ghost that was haunting the firehouse. They held a seance in the firehouse and discovered the ghost was the spirit of a former fireman who had passed away and was unhappy with the fact that the new regulations allowed women to be firefighters. The circle worked with the spirit and convinced him that the new regulations were all right and that female firefighters were not such a bad thing. Satisfied, he left and never came back.

Holding a seance for a haunting is a bit trickier than your average seance (if there is such a thing) and should be considered "advanced" work. While it can sometimes be done successfully by right-minded beginners, it is not for the merely curious, and it is not a game. Haunting seances are usually requested when someone—alive or dead—is unhappy with a particular situation, and the needs of the haunted and the haunter must be taken seriously.

The spirits in most haunted places are unfortunate souls who cannot make the break or who have some unfinished business or who, like the sexist fireman, are worried about something regarding their former lives. Even if the spirit causes trouble for the residents by throwing objects around or pushing people or hiding things, it is best not to begin the seance with a confrontational or angry attitude or the assumption that you are dealing with "evil."

At the other extreme is the "friendly ghost" syndrome, which I use to refer to homeowners who consider it chic to have a ghost to spice up parties, impress friends, and make life generally more interesting. A friend who has handled many cases of hauntings eventually became disgusted with the number of clients who had no concern whatsoever for the spirits' needs. She would be hired to contact a spirit haunting a house, because the new owners wanted to know why "strange things" were happening. When she contacted the spirit, she would discover, as is usually the case, that the spirit really wanted to leave but was having trouble doing so. Then the owners, if they were present, would signal her not to help it! They wanted to keep "their" ghost. If you become involved in hauntings, make it clear to the owners ahead of time that you are a true intermediary, representing both sides, the living and the dead. A spirit's desire to move on is always more important than a living person's wish to own a haunted house.

You should, however, honor the owner's religious beliefs if possible. Before you take a case, ask the owners what they believe about death, the dead, spirits, the next life, and what religious tradition they belong to. If the spirit wants the owners to help it move on by praying for it or performing some ritual to release it, you should ask the owners how they could participate comfortably without violating their own beliefs and practices. On the other hand, some owners do not want to be present at the seance or the follow-up rituals. They may even leave the house and let you take care of the whole thing.

Before you begin the seance, you may want to walk through the house, especially the rooms where the spirit has been encountered. Feel the energy and try to pick up any signs or psychic impressions that may help you.

Begin your seance as you would a seance in your living room. You can use a table already in the house or bring your own. Try to set it up in the room where the spirit most often "appears." Arrange your sitters. Complete your relaxation and meditative exercises. Say your prayers or invocations. Then ask the spirit to come forward and make itself known. Create an open and tolerant atmosphere, just as you would do ordinarily. Nine times out of ten the spirit is not malicious or harmful but misguided or frightened.

Find out what the spirit needs, why it is there, what you as a group or an individual can do to help the spirit. In some cases the spirits need prayers from the living to encourage them to continue their journey into the next world. They may need forgiveness from someone in the house or reassurance that some special concern or task of theirs is going to be taken care of. The typical haunting spirit is not sufficiently evolved to let go of the things that concerned it here on earth; in this sense it is a lower spirit, and we should approach it with compassion, goodwill, and a sincere desire to help.

For example, there was a case of a family who sensed a spirit haunting the fireplace in their living room. The owners of the house "felt" that it was a young girl in her teens. A team of mediums confirmed that the spirit was a teenage girl who had died in the house in the early nineteenth century. (Later, town records were checked, and indeed an adolescent girl had lived and died in the house in the early 1800s.) As it turned out, the girl had been raped, become pregnant, suffered a miscarriage, and then burned the aftereffects in the fireplace. She had kept all this secret from her family. The trauma had so debilitated her that she had died shortly afterward. But she would not completely leave the scene of her tragedy until a team of mediums talked her through her grief and helped her move on.

The procedures for setting up and structuring a seance session are very personal and should reflect your own meditative and ceremonial style. Use the suggestions in this chapter to get going, but be ready to adapt them to the uniqueness of your own group and the circumstances of any special occasion. The most important ingredient is always to conduct each session with respect for the spirits, the sitters, and yourself.

⚜ 6 ⚜
WHEN SPIRITS COME

HOLLYWOOD MOVIES HAVE DEPICTED SEANCES in such dramatic and gothic ways that real people conducting real seances are often disappointed at how subtle spirit manifestations can be. Ingrained in our imaginations is the semi-darkened room suddenly chilled by a blast of cold wind, the few dim lights flickering out, the table lifting off the floor, the medium slumping over, her eyes rolling in their sockets, and an eerie voice speaking from what sounds like a deep, hollow, unearthly cavern. Everyone shivers.

This is not the way it usually happens.

If you sit around a table waiting for this type of phenomena, you may wait the night away and miss the real attempts by spirits to make their presence known. On some occasions the indications of spirits' presence are more dramatic than others, but a wise medium knows the full range of signs and can read the subtle ones as well as those that are flashier. In this chapter we will look at the physical manifestations of spirits, the ways to identify spirits, the kinds of questions to ask, and how to evaluate the answers. Last, we will explore apparitions.

PHYSICAL MANIFESTATIONS

A change in room temperature, a wind or breeze that appears from nowhere, an odor or scent that was not present before, the table creaking, rocking, or tilting—these are legitimate signs that spirits are in the room. They are often not as dramatic, however, as the movies portray them. Once at a seance held in December in New York State almost everyone in the room smelled the scent of roses, yet there were no flowers or rose-scented candles there, nor was anyone wearing rose perfume. The fragrance simply materialized during the moments when the spirit was most active. It was the spirit's way of telling us he was there.

Table movements can be strong, weak, or nonexistent. In some seances the table tilts quite noticeably, possibly with all four legs rising off the floor; at other sittings it may shake almost imperceptibly or creak or pop or jerk a few times and then never move again. The same is true of the room temperature. Spirits do not have to lower the room temperature when they arrive. The notion that spirits love a cold, meat-freezer environment is mythical. In fact some mediums and sitters get quite warm during seances. What's important is to notice any temperature change, no matter how subtle, and when you do, concentrate carefully on the spirit activity that might accompany the change.

Monitor your bodily sensations as well, particularly in your arms and hands. They may become warmer or cooler. A tingling sensation or what feels like a current of energy may run down your arms or across your palms as they lie on the table. Some sitters feel their hands or other parts of their bodies grow heavy or numb. Your hands may stick to the table or sink into the surface slightly and feel as if they cannot be moved easily. Only practice and experience will teach you how to tell the difference between the changes that normally occur in your skin and muscles when you hold your arms in a fixed position for a length of time and the sensations that indicate the presence of spirits. Physical sensations do not have to be felt for you to have a meaningful seance, although it is rare that some members of a successful circle do not experience some type of sensory sign. It has been said that the spirits use physical signs to get our attention and to announce their presence, but physical occurrences are not crucial to the seance. If you are just beginning your practice and these types of physical manifestations do not occur, don't assume that things are going wrong. Just be patient and wait.

In some cases a spirit may give a physical sign of its presence *after* a seance. A medium once told me that spirits sometimes leave messages on her answering machine or give her a phone call shortly after a seance. When she told me this, I was somewhat skeptical. However, I attended one of her seances, and after it was over, the phone rang. The host picked up the receiver, but there was no one on the line. Since the machine was equipped to recall the number of the party who last called, the host entered the code. No number appeared on the screen. Apparently the call had not been placed from another phone. The medium was convinced (and so was I) that it had been the spirit present that evening, giving us one last sign that he was truly there.

The goal of a seance is to receive intelligent communications. Physical phenomena by themselves do not ordinarily convey any meaningful message. If physical signs occur and they seem to be random and meaningless, the spirits may be experimenting with conditions in the room or testing to see how the sitters will respond to the physical phenomena before the spirits present information. Again, be patient and let the events unfold slowly and naturally.

A LIFE CUT SHORT

John and Alicia consulted a medium to inquire into the tragic death of their sixteen-year-old son, Sean, who had been killed in a car wreck seven months previously. His parents were plagued by two questions: had Sean made a successful entry into the next world, and why had fate so cruelly denied him a long, full life? He had been an A student, had enjoyed sports, and had had a passion for the outdoors. He had hoped to make a career in wildlife management.

The parents met with Lydia, a well-respected medium in their hometown. Although Lydia conducts regular seances with a circle of friends, the couple had requested a private session with her. They met in her living room on a Thursday evening, she sitting in a large overstuffed chair and John and Alicia on the couch. To begin, Lydia asked them to sit back, close their eyes, take a few deep breaths, and relax. She suggested they try to clear their minds of distractions and think about Sean as they remembered him: a happy, ambitious boy who loved life.

Lydia had explained to John and Alicia that she would summon her female spirit guide, Morgan, who would find their son, but that it would be the guide who conveyed Sean's messages to the medium. Lydia in turn would tell the parents what their son had said. Lydia closed her eyes, centered herself, and spoke the name of her spirit guide. "Morgan," she uttered softly. A few moments went by, and she repeated the name. "Morgan." Lydia seemed to grow more relaxed, sinking deeper into the easy chair. Several minutes passed, and Lydia spoke to Morgan. "Good evening, Morgan. Alicia and John are here to contact their son Sean. Sean was killed in February in a car accident. Is it possible to speak with him?"

Lydia paused. "Yes, we'd like that," she said. A few more moments went by. "Yes, thank you, Morgan. Tell Sean his parents are here and that they love and miss him." A few seconds passed, then she said to Alicia and John, "Sean is happy that you came here tonight. He knows you've been sad and distraught over his leaving. Do you want to ask him anything?"

Alicia asked, "Sean, are you OK where you are?"

"Yes," replied Lydia, "Morgan says that Sean is happy and content."

"We feel like we never had a chance to say good-bye," said Sean's father. "It's been awful not being able to tell you all the things we'd like you to know."

"Morgan says that Sean knows how you feel, but not to worry about that because he is allowed to keep in touch with you."

"Keep in touch? What does that mean?" asked Sean's mother.

Lydia relayed the question to Morgan, who answered, "Sean's assignment right now is to learn more about himself and human life by being aware of what is happening in his former family. Morgan says that Sean is not really dissociated from the rest of you but that his spiritual development is still linked with you and your other children. He will continue to discover the meaning of some of the questions he used to ask while alive by watching your lives unfold."

The seance proceeded for about twenty minutes with John and Alicia asking many questions, some of which Sean answered through Morgan, others explained by Morgan to help the couple understand what life in the spirit realms was like and what was happening to Sean. Sean assured the couple that his life on earth had not been meaningless just because it was short. "Since I arrived here, I know that I really had learned everything I needed to learn while I was alive," he said. "I was confused for a little while after the accident, but then I was amazed to realize that I really did not need to be in my body anymore. I can progress much faster in the spirit world."

Finally Morgan said that Sean was taken from the family first so that he could be a psychopomp for other family members when it came time for them to die. "This is not unusual," Morgan explained. "Often the first members of a family to die are the ones who meet the others at the time of their deaths and help them make the passage into the next world." Morgan also instructed the parents to pray to Sean, not for him, and that he would hear their prayers and in various ways he would let them know that he was still with them.

At this point Lydia said that both Sean and Morgan had to go and that the parents should say good-bye, which they did. "Sean and Morgan also say good-bye," Lydia added. Then she thanked the two spirits. After a few moments, quietly breathing and relaxing, Lydia came out of her trance and opened her eyes. Then she and Sean's parents spent a few moments discussing what had transpired.

IDENTIFYING SPIRITS

The issue of identifying spirits by name causes considerable controversy among mediums and spiritualists. As Allan Kardec pointed out more than a century ago, "Spirits do not bring us letters of introduction, and it is well known with what facility some of them take borrowed names." He also remarks that "in many cases, absolute identity is a secondary question, and without real importance." And yet mediums and sitters continue to argue and debate the necessity for and methods of making positive identifications.

Obviously if a spirit claims to be a specific person known to a sitter, such as an uncle or a grandmother and reasonable evidence is presented that the spirit is who it says it is, the circle is reassured that the exchange between the sitter and spirit is legitimate and meaningful. Certainly a sitter would be less likely to accept information at face value from a spirit whose identity was in serious question. But it is not always easy to get a positive identification. Some spirits have never been incarnated and consequently have no mortal name or identity to give us. To grill such a spirit about who he or she is or was in an earlier life is fruitless and may annoy or offend the spirit. To complicate matters, some spirits prefer to remain anonymous for reasons that are beyond our ken. A spirit does not have to lay out its résumé to instruct us in the mysteries of the universe.

Assuming a spirit does present itself as a relative or friend of one of the sitters, how can you go about establishing this claim? The general practice is to ask questions that only the spirit would know the answers to, while watching for both answers and personality traits that resemble the person in question. You might ask what its mother's maiden name was or where such-and-such was kept in the house or what happened on a certain occasion when that person was present. One of the pitfalls of this process, however, is that an impostor could give accurate answers by reading the mind of the sitter.

What type of spirits want to fake another's identity? Usually only tricksters or low-level spirits enjoy this ruse and the confusion it can cause. Fortunately, they are neither numerous nor powerful, and they can usually be kept at bay by the sitters' intention and conduct. The energy field of a seance conducted in a high moral tone and with great seriousness of purpose becomes an unwelcome environment for fraud. Tricksters are also attracted to circles that invoke the spirit of a famous person out of curiosity or for fun. Sending out an invocation for a famous person is like advertising for all the "Elvis impersonators" in the spirit world to audition!

A few reasonable questions to establish the trustworthiness of a spirit are not out of line. Most spirits do not mind being questioned, for after all, they want to be believed and respected for who they are. But it is bad form to press a spirit for information more stringently than you would a person still alive. After all, we believe most people when they tell us who they are. The same approach should be taken with most spirits. Do not ask them questions you would not ask them were they still among the living.

When a spirit claims to have lived in a particular town, at a certain address, in a given year, you can try to verify its identity through town records or the local historical society. Anytime after the seance you can visit a site that a spirit might allude to and see if it matches the description the spirit gave. This type of detective work appeals to people who need a greater degree of certainty before believing the content of a spirit's message; most sitters dispense with such earthly concerns once they realize that the spirits' messages are much more interesting than their identities.

"Good" and "Bad" Spirits

Mediums begin seances by explicitly invoking only good or helpful spirits. The circle's intention and purpose, its own moral qualities, and the protection of the medium's and sitters' spirit guides and guardians will generally keep unwanted spirits away. Occasionally, however, a "bad" spirit will show up.

I am qualifying *bad* intentionally here as a reminder that our moral judgments about the spirit world may be grossly mistaken. Even in everyday life we often misjudge others, overlooking the positive aspects of situations, blinded to the bigger picture in which the "bad" events or people play an important role. I might get stuck in a slow grocery line, for example, and start to fume over being late, but on the way home I discover that a serious automobile accident occurred just minutes before I arrived at a dangerous intersection. If the grocery line had moved more quickly, would I have been the injured driver? You are turned down for a promotion at work, but would the extra responsibilities have had a harmful effect on your family life? The web of existence is too intricate and complex for us to evaluate with certainty all the vicissitudes and disappointments of life. We should be circumspect in making moral judgments about goodness or badness, both in this world and in the next.

Nevertheless, bad or harmful spirits do exist; and for reasons not always clear to us, they are allowed to enter our lives and our circles. Although they may be playing an important and ultimately beneficial role in our spiritual evolution, we should assume that it is reasonable to avoid or shun what we perceive as harmful. Therefore we need to know how to recognize bad or harmful spirits and how to get rid of them.

In general we evaluate spirits as we would living people. We can make reasonable judgments based on their language, their interests, their conduct, and what they say. The spirits themselves tell us that the higher spirits cannot do harm and that their messages and conduct are always of the highest moral order. Lower spirits, mischievous spirits, and harmful spirits reveal their true nature by what they say and how they say it. A spirit that is offensive or insulting is probably one you would not want to have around.

Higher spirits are free of anger, hatred, jealousy, and violence. They neither express such qualities in their messages nor encourage these responses in us. If a spirit encourages violent or destructive emotions in us, our suspicions should be aroused that the spirit is not of a high moral order. Be suspicious even of "righteous anger," which is rooted in a deep love for justice and fairness. Acting out of anger, even justifiable anger, is always dangerous because anger is seldom a controllable emotion. It frequently grows beyond reasonable bounds, becoming vindictive and disproportionate to the cause that triggers it. Higher spirits will not feed even righteous anger but instruct us in alternative solutions to injustice.

Intelligence is not a sign that the spirit belongs to the higher moral realms. Some of the most sadistic criminals have had extremely high IQs. Cleverness, a quick wit, insight, and extensive knowledge of business, art, or science do not preclude a warped mind. In fact brilliance can mask an unsavory character. Never become overly impressed by the intelligence of the spirits who instruct you or blinded by erudite explanations and advice. Trust your deeper instincts, look into your heart, and ask for guidance from what some people call your higher self when you suspect that a spirit's influence in your life is less than desirable.

Good spirits do not flatter our egos by telling us what we want to hear. Their praise is grounded in truth and honesty. If they are ignorant about a matter or they are not allowed to reveal certain information, they will remain silent or admit they do not know. A benevolent spirit will never *demand* or *command* us to do something or not to do something. Higher spirits are not sent to take over our lives and strip us of our autonomy. They merely offer advice and suggestions. Good spirits operate with a sense of decency that will appear natural and instinctive to us.

Evaluating the character of spirits is not always easy. Human beings are always prone to self-deception. Therefore we should be humble in admitting that we could be deceived, not just by wicked spirits but also by our own perceptions and standards. Bad spirits are encouraged by our ability to fool ourselves. Seek advice from friends, spiritualists, and other mediums if you have any doubts about your visionary experiences or the spirits you encounter in those experiences.

To free yourself from troublesome spirits, take the following steps. First, call upon your good spirits and contacts. The loving energy of helpful spirits can intimidate harmful spirits into leaving. Second, insist that the unwanted spirit leave immediately. Accept no messages from it. If it does not leave immediately, stop the seance and begin later. Third, be calm and patient. Eventually the disrupting spirit will realize that it cannot provoke you into being upset. You can outwait the spirit; before long he or she will become discouraged and stop interfering in your seances. Always remain in control of your highest thoughts and operate from the highest moral values to show the spirit that you are in control of yourself and, ultimately, of the seance.

Spirit Memories

When trying to determine the identity of a spirit claiming to be a close friend or family member, we would obviously ask questions only that person could have answered, but what should we assume if the spirit cannot answer or answers incorrectly? You have to evaluate each situation on its own merits, keeping in mind that spirits cannot always recall everything about their former lives. Death does not bestow on us total recall of everything that has ever happened to us. We know that some spirits spend a certain amount of time immediately after death in a kind of fog or confused state, perhaps not realizing that they have died. Some emerge from this state quickly, others more slowly. It's possible that making this transition requires some memories to be released, just as the material aspects of life must be released.

It is not clear to us why spirits do not recall certain things. They are not given universal knowledge after death, although they seem to know "more" than we do or more than they did before they died. They receive what we might call "limited" universal knowledge, that is, a greater insight into the mysteries of Creation, a certain wisdom denied us while on Earth. But from what spirits themselves report, they do not "know everything," nor can they recall everything that happened to them in this last life. Some spirits have said that they have the *ability* to recall very minute details of their former lives, but they see no reason for doing so. Although we may think it is important to recall as much as possible (or certain incidents), spirits may view such memories very differently. It is also possible that the amount of energy required for remembering some earthly events is so great that spirits prefer not to use it for that.

Of course spirits seem to recall quite easily the people, places, and events that most influenced their spiritual growth and development. After all, this is the reason we are incarnated: to grow spiritually and evolve into higher beings. Life is a process of transformation. Spirits may "forget" incidents that contributed nothing or very little to their transformation. It is important to remember that we are not in a good position to evaluate the events of another's life. What we think are major events might be of minor importance, their real significance known only to the person concerned and only after he or she has passed over to the other side.

We also have to consider, as mentioned earlier, that time and place are different in the spirit world. Our human concepts of time and place reflect the unique conditions of life on earth. Even life on another planet would give us different perceptions of time, since the cycles of day and night and the seasons of the year would be drastically different or nonexistent. Depending on where we are on earth, we experience time and place differently. Time within the arctic circle and our sense of place on the ice fields would disorient most people familiar only with time and place in a more temperate zone.

We don't know how a particular spirit focuses on events that took place on earth. Dates and places may not be accessible to him or her during a seance. Spirits may see things in broader sweeps of time or in earth time intertwined with time dimensions from other universes or past lives. On the other hand, a spirit may experience time in smaller segments that are rewoven into entirely different time references than we can imagine.

So it may not be easy for a spirit to answer what seems

to us to be a reasonable question, such as "Do you remember the party I threw for you when you turned twenty-one?" The party may have been a major event in your relationship with that person but very insignificant from the spirit's point of view. In fact the spirit's entire twenty-first year may pale in comparison to some briefer event at some other period in life that we know nothing about but that was a major moment of enlightenment or spiritual transformation. So for many reasons we should not immediately assume that a spirit who cannot answer all our questions about its identity is an imposter.

Fading Personality Traits

Using personality traits and speech characteristics is also not a foolproof method for determining a spirit's identity. Spirit teachings over the last century indicate personality traits fade as spirits evolve and journey farther beyond the earthly realms. The natural course of development involves losing many of the personality traits associated with a particular incarnation. While spirits never lose individuality, they do become more uniform, resembling the purer energy of which they (and we) are made as they evolve toward the Creator and the original energy of Creation. A spirit who has recently passed over, however, is more likely to retain the personality traits and speech mannerisms that he or she had in this last life.

The spirits who instructed Allan Kardec also teach that, as they evolve, they form groups or families of spirits who resemble each other in significant ways, such as similar past life experiences, similar missions, the same levels of development. These spirits may resemble each other in personality types as well and cluster into tribes or clans of spirits who currently share a similar existence in the afterlife. Curiously, different spirits within a particular group may use the same name when appearing at seances, even though they are not the same spirit.

Spirits make an effort to appear to us in ways that we will be able to understand; if they did not, they would defeat their purpose. Even spirits who have never been incarnated on earth may use a historic name when invoked so that we have some means by which to identify them.

For example, the name given by a spirit may be a historic name that has particular meaning for us. A spirit may say he is Socrates, not because he is the actual spirit of Socrates but because the class of spirits he belongs to at the moment is characterized by the wisdom that we would recognize as Socrates. Another example of how the spirits try to meet us halfway might be as follows. If a spirit intended to instruct me about nature and wildlife, and it knew that I would pay attention to teachings from Henry David Thoreau (the nineteenth-century American poet and naturalist whom I have always admired), it might use "Thoreau" as its name for communicating with me. For all practical purposes I should probably assume that it *is* Thoreau. But if I question the spirit about Thoreau's life (using details that I have read in biographies), the spirit might not be able to answer because he is not the *historical* Thoreau. Most spiritualists agree that the crucial evidence is in the teachings, not in the name or the identity. If the wisdom and truths that come from "Thoreau" seemed in character with what the historical Thoreau would teach, I would accept them. As always, I would evaluate what I was told after the seance and not assume that just because information or advice comes from a spirit I have to accept it as truth.

Some spirits have taught us that a substitute spirit can be sent in place of another. A circle of sitters may, for example, routinely contact a spirit named Dean. But if

Dean is part of a family of spirits, he might send another spirit on an occasion when he cannot come personally. The substitute will say that he is Dean, and the circle will most likely assume that it is, since the instructions will be in keeping with other communications from Dean.

So if a spirit claiming to be a good friend has lost some of its personality traits or is evolving into a clan of spirits with higher, more etheric traits than she had on Earth, she may not be able to convince you beyond all doubt that she is who she says she is. It may be the exact spirit; it could be a fellow "tribesman" substituting for the friend; or it might be some other type of manifestation unknown to us. You must evaluate the spirit on the strength of its moral tone, its wisdom, and the apparent truth of its messages, as you would similar information from someone living.

Impostors

For the reasons cited so far, identifying spirits posing as other people can be quite difficult. There are no foolproof methods of detection that work in every case. Only practice, sensitivity, and discernment will alert you to impostors, those spirits whose primary goal is to deceive. A higher spirit has no desire to trick you and can be recognized by the high ethical tone and seriousness of its answers to questions. Impostors are found only among some lower spirits, who can usually be spotted by language and messages that are insulting, argumentative, or unethical.

As suggested earlier, recently departed spirits whose characters and personality traits are still strong can often be identified by those who knew them while alive. Their manner of speech, the specific information they have, their personal characteristics and habits all indicate that they are who they say they are (provided, of course, they are not getting this information by reading the minds of the sitter who is asking the questions, which is always a possibility). Much of this type of evidence, however, comes during the session itself, rather than in a "twenty-questions" period at the beginning of the seance, which many spirits find offensive and tend to view as an attitude of suspicion and distrust on the part of the medium and sitters. It is best to give the spirit the benefit of the doubt and go ahead and begin the communication or dialogue. Evidence that the spirit is an impostor will arise as the session proceeds. Watch carefully to see if the thoughts, ideas, sentiments, and moral tone of the spirit match the person as he or she was when alive.

If you have serious doubts about a spirit's identity and cannot continue without clearing them up, you can always resort to a method that mediums have used for many generations. Stop the communication, explain to the spirit that you are having difficulty believing that it is who it says it is, and ask it to affirm its identity in the name of the Creator or Supreme Being or All That Is Good and Holy. A refusal to do so can be presumed to indicate an impostor. But as Allan Kardec pointed out, a lying spirit who is truly unscrupulous might swear anyway.

If you realize you are dealing with an impostor, ask your spirit guide to say good-bye to the impostor, then inform the deceiving spirit that its messages will no longer be relayed to you. If you are channeling directly from a spirit and not using your spirit guide, say good-bye, wish the spirit well, firmly tell it not to return, and end the seance. Take a break and resume later.

GUIDELINES FOR ASKING QUESTIONS

Clear, concise, unambiguous questions stand the best chance of receiving clear, concise, unambiguous answers.

Some circles prepare their questions in advance, before they sit, so that the queries are clearly worded, stating exactly what the sitters want to know. A list of written questions can keep you on track and help you remember what you wanted to ask (it is easy to forget some important question as the seance proceeds). Sometimes the spirits anticipate our questions. When this happens, the leader can check off a question when it gets covered so you don't ask it again. A list of questions is a particularly good idea if you have been working with the same spirits over a period of time and they are instructing you about spiritual development. You will want to avoid inadvertently asking the same questions you asked in previous sessions; you'll want your questions to build on each other from session to session. And with a written list, you'll know which questions don't get answered in one sitting so you can ask them in the next.

In general you should not be overly worried about whether your questions are appropriate. Spirits respond to your intentions and character and will answer questions about good-hearted concerns. Nevertheless, you should try to avoid questions that are silly, impertinent, or arise out of self-centered curiosity or vanity. Here are some basic questions that usually get the seance off to a good start:

- Is anyone there who wishes to communicate with us?
- What name should we call you?
- Have we communicated with you before?
  (If yes, ask when or on what occasions.)
- Do you have a message for someone in particular?
  Who is it?
- Have you come on your own, or have you been sent to us by a higher spirit?

- Were you previously incarnated on earth? Can you tell us when and where you lived?
- Is a relative of one of the sitters trying to reach him or her?

Here are some examples of the kinds of questions the spirits find inappropriate:

- Are you a famous person?
- Can you name the book I was reading last night?
- Are you friends with any of my deceased relatives?
- Can you advise me on a decision I have to make about my career?
- You say you were alive during the French Revolution. Well, who was the famous revolutionary who was killed in his bathtub?

Spiritual development and transformation govern the relationship between the spirit world and our world. The Divine Spirit allows communication between the living and the dead to advance our understanding of ourselves, the universe, the divine mysteries of life and death. For this reason spirits will answer questions about their current condition, other universes, life in the beyond, and the possible fates that await us after death—*provided it is for our good to know this information.* If we ask such questions seriously and not just out of idle curiosity, they will answer, and we can draw comfort and encouragement from what they tell us.

This type of information is not the same as personal issues arising out of vanity or selfishness. For the most part spirits are not impressed with our worldly success or lack of it. Material rewards, riches, fame, and power in this life strike the higher spirits as frivolous and ultimately of little worth. So questions asked from pride or self-interest may or may not receive serious answers.

Some people want to use seances for fortune-telling or divination about the future. But in general spirits do not come to satisfy our curiosity about political elections, horse races, future mates, or winning the lottery. Events such as these seem important to us but not to those who have left this earth. In fact a spirit who seems overly eager to give information about your personal future or fortune is probably a lower spirit who gets a kick out of catering to people's credulity. Occasionally, however, a spirit may reveal something about a future event, especially if it holds important significance for a sitter. For example, a spirit might feel it would be advantageous for a person to change careers or relocate, so it will plant a seed in the person's mind by saying that it sees the person pursuing a certain type of work in the future or living in a certain area of the country. Such insights are usually to nudge us toward the paths that are best for our ultimate spiritual development. This type of information is always of much greater importance than "fortune-telling" information (which is generally about luck rather than choice) and tends to strike us more profoundly, as it involves our own growth.

It seems to be a law of the universe that the Creator does not want us to know too much about the future. There is a purpose for the earth's unique space/time framework. If we were meant to know the future, the Creator could have easily figured out some arrangement by which we would know with more certainty what lies ahead. But that is not the case. Probably if we knew our futures, we would not focus on the present, where our lives are meant to be lived. To understand this we might consider an analogy. Our senses filter out as many stimuli—or more—as they let in. If we were continually aware of all the sights, sounds, smells, and activities going on around us, we would be overwhelmed. The limitations placed on our ability to know the future may play an equally important role.

Many mediums prefer that sitters ask their own spirit guides about personal matters rather than invoke unknown spirits for this or ask personal questions of spirits who have come for other purposes. Our guides and guardians take a keen interest in our lives. Their involvement in our destines is part of their own spiritual evolution. If we must ask about our future or the wisest course of action, we should ask our familiar spirits, rigorously avoiding frivolous questions or ones that arise sheerly out of vanity and self-interest.

Whatever advice we do receive needs to be evaluated carefully, just as we would evaluate advice and suggestions from a friend, a colleague, or even a psychiatrist. The spirits are not our shrinks, personal psychics, or gypsy fortune-tellers. Nor does the advice they give always point to an appropriate course of action, due to variables of which we—or the spirit—are unaware. This is especially true of information that is time-specific. As we have already noted, a spirit's sense of time may be out of sync with ours. Our time frames may have little meaning or be totally meaningless from his or her perspective. This may be why spirits are often reluctant to give specific dates about future events (if they bring up future events at all). For example, if a spirit seems to be telling you that your decision to move to New Mexico is right because he sees you thriving there, he might not realize that your decision is to move this year, and the information he has is about your future ten years from now. It might be that to move to New Mexico this year would be a disaster.

Questions about past and future lives can be asked, but most of us are not meant to know much about them.

Again, the Creator apparently wants us to live this life on its own merits, without a lot of background about our past and future incarnations. Only when it will contribute in an important way to our transformation and evolution do the spirits fill us in on these matters and then only in rather broad, general terms. Be wary of spirits who give a lot of detail about your past lives. They are probably frivolous spirits who enjoy feeding on the vanity of gullible sitters and who may offer outlandish accounts that are not in any way true.

Occasionally a question will be met with silence. What might this mean? Several things could be occurring. The spirit may not have the information at hand but is searching for it or trying to access it, and it will come later. It's possible the spirits simply don't know the answer and for some reason do not indicate that they don't know. They just remain silent.

Try rewording your question a few times or rethink the motives behind the question and ask again. If you still get no answer, it might be that you have asked for information that cannot be revealed at the present time. You can ask, "Is this something you don't know or can't tell me?"

CONTRADICTORY MESSAGES

Contradictions can arise in communications from the otherworld. A spirit's descriptions of life on the other side, its existential condition, the laws of the universe, and other cosmic realities may not compare with similar descriptions from other spirits. Furthermore, even mediums and spiritualists do not always agree on the nature of spirits or life after death or even on the nature of mediumship itself. How can we account for these discrepancies?

Skeptics and unbelievers use contradictions as evidence that seances are hoaxes and that spirit messages are fantasies concocted by mediums and gullible believers. They argue that if there were a life after death and communication with the dead were possible, there would be agreement on basic details. Since consistency is often lacking, it all must be a hoax.

Spiritualists, however, while they may be dismayed and often discouraged by the lack of agreement, do not see this as evidence that spirits do not exist. There are logical and reasonable explanations for contradictions, although they may not be strong enough to convince the hardened skeptic. Let's take a look at some of these.

When one surveys the voluminous literature channeled from the spirit world over the last 150 years or longer, there is remarkable consistency about the basics. For example, the human spirit survives and continues to evolve; there are various ranks or levels of spirits; some of the dead continue to take an interest in the lives of the living; there is remorse over lost opportunities to live better lives and over any harm done in this lifetime; there is great joy at the good done in life; there are opportunities after death to make up for "lost time" and to better one's condition; there is a Creator; and so forth. On matters such as these, there is great consistency, even though individual details can appear contradictory.

Furthermore, many contradictions are more apparent than real. There are immense numbers and ranks of spirits, and differences in their knowledge and development, so the information they convey to us can be as contradictory and muddled as the reports from a hundred different tourists who traveled through Ireland last year. Each spirit, like each human being on earth, selects what it perceives and may never fully understand it. For example, two visitors to Ireland will notice different plants, landscapes, and people and may return home with opposite experiences. One may say it rains every day; the other will swear it hardly ever rains. Both can be correct. The same is true of spirits describing the world beyond the grave.

We should also consider that some spirits may be ignorant of what they are talking about, just as many of us don't know what we are talking about, even though that doesn't stop us from carrying on a conversation long after it has run beyond our ken. We talk off the top of our heads now and then, make assumptions about things we don't know for sure, and extrapolate from what we do know. This is a perfectly human way of carrying on conversations, and while most people are not consciously trying to deceive, we learn how to take what others say with a grain of salt. There are, of course, some spirits (like some mortals), who intend to deceive. They get pleasure out of lying and sowing confusion. We need to be on guard for these con artists of the spirit world, just as we do for earthly con artists.

Also important is the fact that spirits who instruct us in the mysteries of the universe often tailor their messages for specific sitters. Information often applies only to a particular individual. If a spirit tells me personally, for example, that the spirits of my deceased pets cannot communicate with me, that may or may not be a universal truth about the spirit world. It's possible that it is just *my* former pets who cannot communicate with me (or perhaps they don't want to because they are pouting) and not that the spirits of animals can *never* communicate with their former owners.

In addition, spirits may emphasize certain aspects of their messages because they are important for a particular sitter. For instance, a person may be told that one of the most terrifying things about life after death is remorse over not having spent more time with your family while you were still alive. While that may be universally true in principle, in a particular seance it may be emphasized because the person for whom the message is intended will indeed suffer great remorse over this. But other people may not be as bothered by it. Some people probably should *not* spend more time with their families.

We should also be aware of analogies and not report them to others as fact. For example, in the Western world one of the most common analogies about the next life is that good people go to heaven, where they sit on clouds and play harps. Most likely this description originated as an analogy about heaven being a pleasant place far removed from the problems of earth (and meant to appeal to people who enjoyed harp music). But if you are the type of person who would consider this a perfectly dreadful way to spend eternity, do not despair. Clouds and harps are analogies. Many spirit descriptions employ analogies, and we need to recognize them as such when reporting them to others.

It is also a good idea to be wary about applying personal messages or instructions indiscriminately to other people or, what's even worse, turning them into universal truths applicable to the whole human race. Sadly, channeled information is too often used precisely in this way, and people for whom it was never intended "transform" their lives in ways that are not appropriate for them personally. Messages received through famous media channels have often been overgeneralized and have ruined many people's lives. While all sacred literature is important to the human race, and all channeled information from the spirits is part of the reservoir of human wisdom, not every man or woman is meant to live his or her life in accordance with every scrap of wisdom ever recorded.

An obvious example of this concerns the dietary restrictions that arise in particular religious and cultural contexts. The dietary laws of Judaism, Tibetan monasticism, and Hinduism (to cite only three) are all different. There is no way one individual could satisfy all the religious dietary laws in the world, nor would anyone try. Yet many people take channeled spiritual instructions from widely different sources and try to reconcile them and apply them to their lives.

Another source of inconsistencies is that spirits communicate in terms and concepts that the current generation will be able to understand and accept. In the nineteenth century, for example, many spirit messages speak demeaningly about non-Christians, especially people still living in tribal cultures. Today, through greater contact with native people and a more tolerant attitude in the West, the spiritual customs of native people are becoming highly respected, especially those that affirm the sacredness of nature. Consequently our present attitude does not square with the information of spirit messages recorded in many nineteenth-century seances that perpetuate the myth of Western superiority and the "benighted" ignorance of primitive people.

We need to place the values and attitudes expressed in seances in their cultural context and realize that spirits need to speak in the "spirit of the times" to reveal the greater truths of the cosmos in bite-sized servings that can be consumed and digested by the contemporary generation. Even today the spirits are tempering their messages to make sense to our current level of understanding. A century from now a new generation of mediums will undoubtedly look back in shock at how prejudiced and incomplete our knowledge and wisdom were in the late twentieth century. They may even think we were nuts!

Another thing to remember is that human language is always inadequate to some extent, and yet we have to use it. Spirits may not be able to convey exactly what they intend, any more than we do when we try to describe experiences that are ultimately indescribable or ineffable. Many visionary experiences and cosmic truths defy human words and concepts. Mystics in every culture have felt the poverty of language to convey the rich, powerful, multidimensional quality of their knowledge and experience. We must take the problem of language into account when we receive messages, when we record them in our journals, and when we pass them on to others. If the original message is poorly worded, our retelling or interpretation of it may be that much more so.

APPARITIONS

It is probably best that spirits are not constantly visible and that we are not constantly aware of them. There are so many spirits that their presence would overwhelm us. Spiritualists have said that the Creator does not want us to realize how "crowded" the universe is with conscious beings who take an interest in our lives. We are meant to go through life relying on our own initiative, intelligence, and reason. We are meant to live *as if* we were on our own, even though as many spiritualists believe, we could not survive without the protection and guidance of helping spirits. In many ways this is similar to our not being allowed to know all the truths of the universe or to see our future in clear detail. We are meant to live with limited knowledge and within the constructs of time and space as they are structured in this universe. Consequently, the spirit world remains largely invisible.

Yet spirits do appear to people in highly visible ways. On occasion their "physical" bodies and clothing can be seen and touched. Spirits may have a natural ability to appear visibly, judging from the many accounts of spirits appearing to someone at the moment of death or shortly thereafter, when they would hardly have had time to "learn the ropes" about what can and cannot be done in the spirit world.

For example, in 1985 Dr. Christiaan Barnard, the famous South African heart surgeon who performed the first heart transplant, reported an incident that occurred in his life. At the time of the apparition Barnard was himself a patient in a hospital. At 10:00 P.M. he saw a woman enter his private room wearing a white gown, looking "very thin and pale, with blue eyes and gray hair." She "pressed strongly" on his chest; he pushed her away by grabbing her wrists, which he described as "very fragile." Barnard was amazed at how "extremely light" the woman seemed to be. As he pushed her away, she levitated and left the room through the window. Barnard then rang for a nurse, but it was a few moments before one came, with the apology that she couldn't come immediately because a patient was dying in the women's ward just as he rang. The doctor asked the nurse to describe the woman, and the nurse said she was thin, had blue eyes and gray hair, and was wearing a white nightgown. Barnard was convinced that it was the same woman who had visited him in his room.

It seems that spirits do not lose this ability to materialize in their physical bodies, although how they do so, years after they have died and left those bodies, remains a mystery. From what the spirits have told mediums over the years, all spirits have the ability to appear visually to mortals (though obviously not all of them do so). Some spirits may not have permission to appear; others are in circumstances or in certain stages of development where it is not possible to appear at a particular moment.

The way the spirits look when they reveal themselves probably reflects what we need to see rather than what is "natural" for the spirit. For example, although a spirit does not need clothing, the person to whom it appears will recognize it more readily (and feel more comfortable) if the spirit is clothed rather than naked. Spirits may also appear wearing the type of clothing they wore when alive, even though their clothes would not have survived the centuries. It has been suggested that spirits can influence, to some degree, the elemental energies, particularly light, and transform them into visible matter. We may never know exactly how they do it. What we do know is that they can manifest physically for us whatever we need to recognize them and accept them as real. In fact, many people report seeing spirits who look gauzy or who wear translucent, gossamer gowns (or even have wings); just as with the analogies used in messages, the "costumes and props" of an apparition may be selected with an eye for dramatic effect. A spirit may wish to cater to the beliefs about spirits held by the person to whom it is appearing. For a person who believes that spirits have wings, a spirit might appear with wings. If we believe that everyone is young in the next world, a spirit may appear to us as young and healthy. On the other hand, if you believe that spirits remain at the age they were when they died, then a deceased grandmother may appear to you as the eighty-year-old woman she was when she passed on. Spirits are shape-shifters and often appear in forms that make sense to the mind of the person who sees them.

The physical shape and form of the spirit are determined partially by cultural expectations. In Celtic lands and in Native American societies where some spirits are thought of as "little people," they are often seen as diminutive men and women. In many tribal cultures around the world, spirits appear in animal form because that is how people expect to see them. Even modern, urban Westerners who practice core shamanism (the essential elements of shamanism, stripped of any particular tribal context) will meet a helping spirit in the form of an animal power if they are prepared to do so.

Everyone has the ability to see spirits, although each person may experience this ability in slightly different ways. I recall a friend who was present at a church in Kentucky where a local psychic predicted that the Virgin Mary was to appear on a certain day. Thousands of people came from all over the area. Some saw the Virgin; others did not. Afterwards, I asked my friend, who said she had seen the apparition, whether the Virgin was standing on the floor of the church or hovering in the air. "Oh, I don't know," she replied. "I had my eyes closed."

I firmly believe that my friend saw the Virgin and that the fact that her eyes were closed does not invalidate her experience or suggest that she was just imagining the apparition. Many, if not most, visionary experiences occur with our eyes closed or slightly closed or when we are staring in a transfixed way. Visions often occur under dimly lit conditions—in moonlight, fog, or mist—or when we are quite tired. Seeing spirits with our physical eyes is not important. Visionaries tend to agree that they see with their "inner eye" or "third eye" or with what the Irish call "the Sight." It is not a physical ability but a metaphysical one. When the eyes are open, we might see a bright flash of light, a strange wisp of fog, a sparkling shimmer on the surface of a lake, and *within* this vision of physical reality we perceive a spiritual reality. It's as if ordinary reality is in some sense "hollow," and under the right conditions—with our eyes open or closed; it doesn't matter—we can see the normally invisible realities within.

The same is true of auditory perceptions, what we commonly refer to as "hearing voices." Whether we physically hear them or hear them with our "inner ear," what we perceive is a spiritual stimulus akin to physical sound. Most people are able to hear "voices" in a babbling brook or a waterfall, but not everyone will hear the spirits speaking *within* those voices. Furthermore, a physical sound is not necessary at all. You can hear spirits speaking to you in the strictest silence. As with "the Sight," some kind of altered state of awareness usually accompanies the voices. The visionary/auditory state might be triggered by strange or eerie lighting conditions, fatigue, a mesmerizing sound such as drumming, chanting, or falling water, even by an illness that distorts our perceptions with pain, fever, or boredom.

Apparitions, of course, are not necessary for communication. A spirit does not have to be visible to speak to us or to affect material objects. Even when visible, a spirit may not speak audible words (although it might) but communicate through transmission of thoughts.

MATERIALIZATIONS

Although it is rare, spirits can materialize objects during a seance. They can make physical objects such as furniture, books, dishes, and silverware appear. They can "create" physical atmospheric conditions, such as changing the weather or altering the temperature or scent of a room.

Again, we don't fully understand how this happens, but their ability to do so undoubtedly derives from the same type of energy manipulation with which they materialize their own former bodies. Allan Kardec referred to this feat as "formation, not creation." In other words, spirits do not create physical objects in the same sense that the Creator does. The objects brought into existence by spirits are temporary manifestations arising from the rearrangement of substances and energies already existent, not the creation of objects out of nothing. By concentrating and focusing energy into a particular spot, spirits can make an object appear there. As with other physical manifestations, spirits may use materializations to grab our attention, convince us of their existence, or prove some principle in which they are instructing us.

Many accounts attest to spirits having powers over physical objects and their ability to materialize and even dematerialize objects when it serves some good purpose to do so. For example, a close relative of mine lost a diamond, which she usually wears on a chain around her neck. Formerly it had been on her mother's engagement ring and was therefore a precious keepsake. When she discovered it missing, she thought back to when she had last noticed it and concluded that it must have fallen off as she was coming home from the grocery store. She retraced her steps, checked inside the car, the trunk, the driveway where she had unloaded the bags of groceries, and the kitchen. It was nowhere to be found. She gave particular attention to searching the driveway, because she thought the necklace might have torn loose as she carried the grocery bags inside. But the diamond was not there. Quite distraught over the loss, she prayed that night to her deceased daughter to help her find the diamond. The next day when she went out to get the morning paper, she found the diamond lying in the middle of the driveway, shining brilliantly in the morning sun. It was lying right in the open, in the very spot she had searched thoroughly the day before.

Assuming that she hadn't simply overlooked it in her search, which my relative swears is impossible, the next most likely explanation is that her daughter's spirit had answered her prayer. Through some power over material reality that we do not fully understand, the daughter's spirit found the diamond and moved it to a place where she was sure her mother would find it the next day. Whether she physically lifted the diamond and carried it to the center of the driveway or dematerialized it wherever it had been lost and rematerialized it in the driveway we will never know.

An interesting consideration concerning materializations is to what extent we help the spirits bring them about. As we have noted, spirits rely on the group energy of the sitters at a seance to communicate with the living. It's possible that they also require the circle's energies to materialize objects during a seance. In the case of the lost diamond, it's possible that without the woman's heartfelt prayer to her daughter and her strong desire to recover the diamond, the daughter's spirit might not have been able to make the diamond appear in the driveway.

A similar phenomenon occurs every day among the living who have strong powers of concentration. It is often referred to as *projecting, manifesting,* or *visualizing* what you need. If you need something seriously enough, by visualizing the object or the desired condition you help bring it into existence. You project your need or desire out into the universe, where it manifests. It may be that every successful manifestation is partially the work of helping spirits. Skeptics, of course, would say these are sheer coincidences, but from a spiritualist point of view there are no coincidences. There are only synchronicities.

The universe operates on the principle of synchronicity or meaningful, purposeful connections directed by higher powers who take an active interest in our affairs. It may not be difficult to manipulate energies into our range of perception so that they materialize as solid objects. From our earth-bound space/time perspective we may never realize which tasks are hard and which are easy. It may actually be a simpler feat for faith to move mountains than for a finger to move an anthill.

Lack of faith and chronic disbelief prevent us from recognizing synchronicities, but they occur far more often than we realize. People who meditate, pray regularly, or observe their own lives from a spiritual perspective report that synchronicities occur often and when needed. A good practice is to record in a journal before going to bed at night all the "coincidences" that occurred during the day. After a few weeks or so you will be amazed at how many there were and how many fall into the category of synchronicity rather than "just luck."

The synchronistic pattern of our lives suggests that there really is a Divine Power watching over us, a Divine Spirit who operates through the things of Creation and the spirits of Creation. Materializations should not surprise us. The entire universe is a materialization, and the principles and laws of materializing function in ways that may be understandable only through the eyes of faith.

Communicating successfully with spirits is an art that requires considerable practice. Go slowly when information comes; mull it over after the seance, confer with friends if necessary, and reflect on all the possible outcomes and consequences that might occur if you follow a spirit's advice. Always keep in mind that a spirit's message may not be appropriate for you in precisely the way you interpreted it. It may have simply been offered to get you thinking along new lines, awaken you to new possibilities, or encourage you to reevaluate your present life.

The best mediums and sitters are humble, sensitive, and respectful toward the spirits that come, realizing that seance work plays an important role in our development and progress as human beings. After all, that is why spirits come: to teach, enlighten, and assist us in our paths through this world and into the next.

๙ 7 ๙

HEALING SEANCES

THE WIFE OF A PROFESSOR AT THE UNIVERSITY OF Arizona was slowly coming out of the anesthesia after an operation for cancer. Her first memory, which she related to her husband as soon as she regained consciousness, was that during the surgery a group of old Indian men had been standing around the operating table. She had had an odd sense that they were helping her pull through the operation. Later she learned that a Native American healer, whom she had gone to several months previously for a healing ceremony, had called on the spirits of sixty-four medicine men to watch over her. According to Apache tradition, the medicine men guard the sick and help them through their illnesses.

Tribal cultures traditionally have a much closer rapport with the spirit world than modern Western societies, and shamans and native healers frequently invoke the power of the spirits to assist the ill and the dying in their struggles for health. Today Westerners are turning in increasing numbers to native healing traditions, when they are available, to supplement Western medicine, discovering in those ancient techniques a remarkable approach to holistic health and wholeness. We are learning that regaining and maintaining our health requires mental, emotional, and spiritual remedies as well as physical ones.

Yet we don't have to turn to different cultures to find spiritual methods for healing. There are strong healing traditions within Western culture that are often overlooked because they have been disparaged by mainstream medical practitioners. These include faith healing, laying on of hands, and psychic healing, each of which can be performed in the context of the seance, enhanced by the energy of a circle of supportive people.

THE DIFFERENCE BETWEEN CURING AND HEALING

First, we should be clear about the difference between curing and healing. *Curing* means eliminating a disease or an illness so that the physical body returns to its former state. *Healing* means bringing the entire person—body, mind, and spirit—into a state of harmony and balance, a condition that does not require the curing of the disease. In fact, curing the disease by itself does not guarantee health on a holistic level. Let's take a look at some examples of this.

Chemotherapy may cause cancer to go into remission; a heart bypass may eliminate pain and restore a proper flow of blood to the heart; spinal surgery may allow a person to walk again. In a purely physical sense these Western methods "cure" the disease. The patient, however, may not be healed by them. The cancer patient may continue to live in fear of the cancerous cells returning; the bypass patient may not adjust to the notion that she will have to live with a huge scar on her chest; the man with the back operation may feel "less a man" because he can no longer engage in sports and the strenuous life that formerly played an important part in his self-identity. In other words, mending the physical body does not always bring a patient to a state of wholeness, of feeling complete and healthy on all levels of one's being.

Even more discouraging are the illnesses for which Western medicine can do nothing. To live with terminal cancer, AIDS, incurable paralysis, or diabetes, monitoring and adjusting your lifestyle accordingly, requires great reservoirs of mental, emotional, and spiritual energies. The *person* must be strong and healthy, especially if the body is not. In these situations, where curing is out of the question, healing is absolutely necessary.

There are various approaches to healing the whole person as opposed to curing the disease, and the ones that tend to be the most effective have two features in common: community and ceremony.

THE SEANCE AS COMMUNITY AND CEREMONY

Studies in holistic health, especially those focused on lingering diseases such as cancer, AIDS, diabetes, and various addictions, indicate that healing takes place most effectively in a context of community and ceremony. These are the key ingredients of many native healing methods, and they are two components of traditional seances. A seance can be a healing ritual in which family, friends, and well-wishers participate for the sake of bringing a person's body, mind, and spirit into harmony and balance.

From a holistic point of view, illness itself is a result of a person falling out of balance and harmony with himself or herself, other people, the social environment, or the natural world. Many native healers say that disharmony occurs when we lose our spiritual connections with the greater universe and the spirits who guard us and protect our health. When we fall out of sync with the natural rhythms and harmonies of the universe, our own personal dimensions—physical, mental, emotional—fall out of sync as well, losing vital energy. The result is often illness or disease.

From a spiritualist point of view the universe is composed of forces or energies tending toward health and wholeness, and it is when we become isolated from those forces that our health deteriorates. Saying that the universe tends toward health and wholeness is not to deny physical deterioration and death. These play an important part in the grander scheme of Creation. But when we live in harmony with the greater cosmic forces of health, we die peacefully, or what traditionally is called a "holy" or "happy" death.

If we want to live with a sense of peace and place in the universe, we cannot ignore the world of divine energy. If we focus our energies solely on the material world, we can grow alienated and dysfunctional even on the physical level. A seance provides a supportive circle of friends and the ritual context in which we can reassert and strengthen our links with the world of spirit and divine energies. For those whose illnesses are incurable, whose physical existences will forever be touched by pain or suffering, contact with the larger environment is necessary for living with a sense of peace and place. In a seance we reach out to the web of life whose threads unite us with All-That-Is and serve as channels through which healing energy flows.

IS FAITH NECESSARY?

The old question about whether faith is necessary for "faith healing" takes on a more subtle twist with information gleaned from recent mind-body studies. In olden days we might have said that faith healing is pointless for someone who doesn't have faith. Today we would probably have to define faith in somewhat different and broader terms than was done a generation or two ago.

Studies have shown that thoughts and emotions affect our state of health. Attitudes and feelings contribute to our state of well-being. Some researchers claim that negative thoughts and feelings cause disease directly, while others suggest that mental and emotional negativity produce stress, which weakens the body and lowers the immune system, creating a ripe field in which disease can flourish. Mental and emotional attitudes influence recovery as well. Here too there are differences of opinion. Whether to fight an illness or resign oneself to a fatal condition is a complicated question. But whether we are fighting to get well or resigning ourselves to the inevitable, we need mental, emotional, and spiritual energy to accomplish our goals. In this sense our beliefs about ourselves, our illnesses, the possibility of recovery, and our ultimate places in the universe contribute to our state of well-being.

In the past, people affected by seances were stereotyped as "suggestible." Only suggestible people, it was said, benefited from a seance. But is this not simply another way of saying our beliefs—woven with thought and feeling— are crucial for healing? If so, then suggestibility and faith are not bad things. But we are still left with the question of whether faith is absolutely necessary. In spite of the evidence that our beliefs contribute to our state of health, it appears that belief in a ceremonial healing is not always

ANGER AND FATIGUE

Stewart, age thirty-five, asked his friend Paul if he could attend Paul's seance group for a healing. Stewart suffered from chronic fatigue syndrome, a mysterious illness that leaves a person tired, achy, and depressed, without energy to do the simplest tasks. Paul talked it over with his circle, and they set up a night for Stewart to join them.

The circle, which called itself Earth Spirit Healing, used several methods for healing, depending on the nature of the client's problem. The members discussed beforehand how to work with Stewart and decided on the following procedure.

Stewart lay on the floor on a blanket, and the seven members of Earth Spirit Healing sat around him in a circle. They held hands for a few moments while each person took two or three deep breaths and relaxed. Penny was the evening's facilitator. (The group did not have a formal leader, although they always met in Ralph's apartment, and he usually took care of setting up sessions, making phone calls, and reminding people of what was coming up.) She began with a prayer, asking the Spirit of Healing to flow through them to reach and heal Stewart in whatever way was appropriate for his own spiritual development. Then the group dropped hands and sat in silence for about five minutes while each person called on his or her spirit guide to be present and active in the evening's session.

Next Penny began shaking a small gourd rattle that the group used to focus their attention and alter their consciousness to be more receptive to spirit power. This kind of gentle sound also helps a client relax and become more receptive to healing. After a few minutes of steady rattling, the circle joined hands, and Penny led them through a

guided visualization to raise energy. She asked them to see
a stream of pale green light coming up from the ground and
a similar stream of pale blue light descending from the sky.
The two energy streams flowed into each person and met in
the heart area, where they formed a blue-green braid of
energy that flowed out of each person's left arm and hand
and into the person on the immediate left. Penny told them
to see the light move faster, filling each member of the
circle, even as it passed through them and around and
around the circle.

When enough time passed for each person to feel
spirit-filled, and for the circle itself to be energized by the
blue-green light of sky and earth energies, Penny instructed
each person to lay hands on Stewart's body and send the
energy into him. Each person continued to visualize energy
coming from above and below, passing into Stewart.

As they were doing the healing work, Stewart heard a
strong voice (which he later said must have been a helping
spirit) tell him it was time to release the anger he felt for
being so tired all the time. He said to the group, "Can you
take the anger I feel out of me?"

"Where in your body is the anger?" asked Penny. "In
my stomach," Stewart replied. Each member of the circle
placed a hand a few inches above Stewart's stomach. "What
color is the anger?" Penny asked. "Brown," he answered.

"Breathe deeply and slowly and send the anger out of
your stomach and into our hands on each exhale," Penny
instructed. Stewart did so, visualizing the brown flow of
anger leaving his stomach, while each member of the circle
saw the brown energy flow into his or her hands. Penny
asked him to tell them when the anger was gone or when he
had released as much as he could that night. In a few
minutes Stewart said it was gone. On a signal from Penny

the circle clapped their hands once, and then each person cupped his or her hands and blew the anger upward into the atmosphere, where it could dissipate and return as neutral energy into the universe.

Then Peter, a circle member, said that during the healing his spirit guide told him an affirmation to give to Stewart. "Ring of energy pass through me/Bringing strength from eternity." Peter's guide told him that Stewart should sing or chant the affirmation several times a day or whenever he felt low.

The group then thanked the spirits that had joined them for the evening, and the healing session was over.

Stewart, although not cured of chronic fatigue syndrome, felt greatly energized, better than he had for months. The effects of the healing session stayed with him for quite some time, and he continued to use the affirmation whenever he felt tired or depressed.

necessary for the ceremony to have a positive effect.

People have been healed, even cured of disease, in ceremonial contexts without believing in the efficacy of the ceremony. Patients have recovered almost miraculously from serious illnesses and doubtful surgeries when others have prayed for them, even though their doctors have given up hope. Studies have shown that it doesn't even seem to matter if the patient *knows* that he or she is being prayed for! A study at a modern hospital showed that those who were prayed for recovered at a faster rate or more successfully than those who were not prayed for. Similarly, skeptics have attended healing circles or gone to healers who lay on hands and have gotten better. We do not know exactly just what mental, emotional, and spiritual dynamics come into play for spiritual and psychic healing to work. Suffice it to say, *something* works. And sometimes it doesn't work. Psychic healing, like Western medicine, is not an exact science.

THREE TYPES OF HEALING

For the sake of clarity we should distinguish among three types of healing: faith, psychic, and spiritual. In actual practice it is not always possible to separate the three because often they overlap. But theoretically a healer may be treating a patient's or client's condition by using one or a combination of these methods.

Faith healing relies on the Divine Power to cure or bring about a healing. The healer calls on God, Goddess, Jehovah, the Great Spirit, or whatever name for the Creator he or she uses. If a cure results, it is attributed to the Divine Power. If the person does not recover or dies, that too is attributed to the Divine Will. In faith healing the patient and healer consign the situation to a Higher Power in the belief that disease and death are part of human existence and therefore have some divine purpose. Not even death is a dead end. On the contrary, suffering and dying are steps in our evolution to higher stages of life and happiness.

Psychic healing is the use of a healer's psychic abilities, such as clairvoyance, clairsentience, or psychokinesis, to diagnose and treat a client. Often a psychic healer diagnoses a condition and prescribes a cure in a trance state, where he or she accesses information through paranormal channels. People who feel generally run down or suffer from an undefined malady might seek a psychic healer to discover what the problem is and perhaps have the healer suggest a cure. For example, a psychic healer may see that a client has diabetes and suggest the person go to a medical doctor for treatment. The prescription might also involve alternative remedies such as drinking a certain type of tea, practicing meditation and relaxation techniques, or receiving some type of body therapy such as massage or reflexology.

Some psychic healers use psychokinetic powers to bring about a cure. Psychokinesis is the ability to affect material objects with the power of the mind, such as moving a book along a tabletop or bending a spoon without touching it. If psychokinesis can move physical objects on a table, there is no reason to suppose that it could not also "move" parts of the physical body. So, for example, a psychic healer might concentrate this power on the tissues of a broken bone to help them mend faster or cause the swelling to go down safely in a sprained ankle. Psychokinesis could shrink or break up a kidney stone so that it passes without difficulty.

Interestingly, psychokinesis is not the explanation most psychic healers offer to describe what they do. Many operate within a spiritual or religious context and attribute their success not to the paranormal powers of their own minds but to the healing energy of the universe or God. They see themselves as channels for that energy. Consequently, psychic healers are often indistinguishable from what we call spiritual healers, who work with the spiritual powers of the universe.

Spiritual healing often refers simply to the transfer or infusion of energy into a person to bring him or her back into balance and harmony. Healing energy is not the same as electromagnetic energy, which can be monitored with the scientific equipment, although many healers say that the two kinds of energy are related to each other. Spiritual healers say that the vital energy comes from God, the greater universe, or helping spirits.

What is the vital energy used in spiritual healing? Many religions and metaphysical systems teach that some type of invisible or etheric energy pervades the universe and that a steady flow of this invisible energy is necessary for life and health. In Polynesia it is called *mana*; in India *prana*; in China *chi*. In many cultures this vital energy is said to be sacred and synonymous with the Divine Spirit of the universe. A spiritual healer's power derives from a personal and intimate relationship with the Divine Spirit or the lesser helping spirits.

SPIRITS AS HEALING GUIDES

Like tribal shamans and medicine people, mediums attribute their healing abilities to their personal healing spirits. They will seek guidance from their spirits in all matters, even regarding whether they should see a particular client. If you are thinking about attempting a healing seance, your spirits will tell you whether you are capable of helping a person and/or whether there is any possible harm for you from working with a given client (such as temporarily taking on the person's symptoms). Your familiar spirit may also provide the diagnosis for clients who do not know what is wrong with their health and suggest prescriptive remedies or healing rituals. Sometimes you (or your spirit guide) can access this information from the client's own helping spirits.

Your spirit guide does not have to be the spirit of a former doctor, nurse, or other health practitioner to be a source of health information. In fact spirits who identify themselves as former physicians are not necessarily more reliable or accurate in health matters than other spirits. As we have noted, some recently discarnate spirits are not any more intelligent or informed than when they were alive, and their medical knowledge may be incomplete, misguided, or just plain wrong. (It remains something of a mystery to us why some spirits know things that others do not.) Since a recently departed doctor or nurse may not be any more accurate than he or she was when alive, you should take great care to evaluate a spirit who claims to have been a medical authority just as you would if you were seeking a doctor in ordinary life. Trust your spirit guides once you know them and their abilities. Be wary of spirits you have never worked with before, even if they claim to have been brilliant physicians.

Keep this in mind if your spirit guide was once a tribal medicine man or woman. It appears that former shamans and medicine people are being assigned to serve as spirit guides for healers who are trying to incorporate holistic techniques, based on the philosophies and procedures of tribal peoples, into their practices. But we must acknowledge the possibility that advice from even the spirits of shamans may be incomplete, prejudiced, or inappropriate in any given case. Being native or tribal is not synonymous with being correct. It just means that the healing methods recommended may be more holistic and spiritually oriented than those suggested by a spirit trained in Western medicine. An ethical medium will strongly encourage clients to seek second and even third opinions from mainstream medical doctors and/or alternative practitioners.

THE HEALING CIRCLE

The same considerations for gathering and running the circle apply to a healing seance as when the goal is simply to contact the spirits of the dead. There are, however, other procedures that might be tried, and we will look at those a bit later.

Healing work is energy work. As we saw earlier, the circle functions in a very important way by creating a strong pool of psychic and spiritual energy. Spirits tap into this energy field to supplement their own supply of energy so they can manifest and communicate with the living. If a circle is planning to channel energy directly to a sitter (or someone not physically present), the consolidated energy of the individual sitters, medium, and helping spirits can bring about a very powerful healing.

Vital energy resides in every created thing, but certain things contain more of it or hold it in greater concentrations. Fresh foods, wild plants and animals, running or falling water, fresh spring water, the wind, fire, crystals, sunlight, and certain stones hold greater concentrations of power and energy. Shamans and native healers usually use sources such as these in their healing rituals. Often they conduct rituals near places of spectacular beauty or power, such as waterfalls, pine forests, or hot springs (here there is a concentration of negative ions, which produce feelings of exhilaration and well-being in people). Vital energy is everywhere, and good healers know how to access it from natural objects and places. However, vital energy can also be raised by a group of people.

Singing, chanting, dancing, drumming, and shaking rattles are exciting and dramatic methods of raising energy. However, many traditional mediums find these too energetic—and noisy—for seances. But silent breathing, meditating, and visualizing also raise power and can fit easily into your regular procedures. The common element in all these methods is that strong emotion and concentrated attention (mental energy) attract and build up vital energy. Anytime people pool their own efforts to raise energy or power from the earth and the atmosphere around them, the results can be truly spectacular.

Maintaining Your Own Health and Energy

Mediums and sitters must not drain their own energy reserves, even if their technique calls for using their own energy. Some healers claim that they do not use their own energy but merely channel energy from the universe. If so, there is no need to be concerned about depleting your own energy reserves. But other healers *do* channel their own energy into a client. For example, Dolores Krieger, the developer of Therapeutic Touch, a method of directing energy through the hands, describes healing as a means of transferring energy from one individual to another.

The key to transferring energy is to remember that you have a limitless supply available to you in the universe. Krieger uses the Indian term *prana*, a reminder that the healing energy we transfer to another, while it may be from our own reserves, is the same energy that pervades the entire cosmos. The trick is to keep your lines open, keep your spirit links strong, and see yourself centered in the great web of life where the energy of the universe can course through each thread, pass through you, and fill the person you are working with.

People react differently to the demands of healing work, just as they do to seances and channeling sessions. Some say they are energized by the experience, while others feel somewhat drained, especially after a particularly intense session. If you begin a healing seance already physically tired, worried, emotionally distraught, or not in the best health yourself, you may experience a drain on your physical, mental, or emotional energies. This may or may not correspond to how you experience the result spiritually; you can be physically exhausted and spiritually revitalized.

The issue of taking on the symptoms of a client's illness is important for mediums and healers just beginning this work. Most healers and mediums detach themselves from the client's symptoms, maintaining clear psychic and spiritual divisions between themselves and their clients, between their own energy fields and those of the people who come for help. It is important to protect your own vital resources from the negative influence of a client, just as you would take precautions not to catch a contagious disease from someone. A common way to do this is to surround yourself with a protective light or color or visualize yourself inside a safe egg or cocoon made up of strong psychic energies. Another method is to maintain firm contact with your helping spirits throughout the session by seeing them, feeling them, and acknowledging their presence.

Interestingly, however, some mediums intentionally take on the symptoms of the person they are helping. In fact this is one method by which you can make a diagnosis. If a medium feels pain in her stomach, she may suggest to the client that he has ulcers or chronic indigestion. A sharp pain in the lower right abdomen may indicate approaching appendicitis. Usually the symptom is only momentary and disappears after the medium leaves the trance. It hardly ever brings on the disease or actual condition in the medium. Nevertheless, wise mediums always surround themselves with healing energies and the protection of their own spirits just to be on the safe side.

A successful channeler whom I will call Tessi related to me the following experience about taking on someone else's suffering. She had been asked to do a series of trance sessions in relation to a murder that had occurred in New York's Hudson River valley. A woman's strangled body had been discovered, but her identity remained unknown. Tessi was asked to try to contact the spirit of the dead woman and learn her identity to help the police with their investigation. The first session revealed little about the woman, although Tessi discovered some important details about the murderer, which later proved to be accurate.

In the second session, however, a remarkable event took place. In trance Tessi felt the spirit of the dead woman come into her, and together they relived the events leading up to the gruesome murder. In addition, repeating the murder gave the unfortunate woman time, before she left her body once again, to experience her death and to grieve for it. Tessi sobbed uncontrollably as the spirit of the woman used Tessi's tears and emotions to release her sorrow. In other words, as Tessi later explained, the seance allowed the woman to heal her death trauma, something she had not had time to do when it actually occurred. Tessi obviously did not die of strangulation, but her experience of it was truly terrifying.

In this case the medium took on the symptoms of a spirit rather than a client, but the point is the same: namely, when dealing with the pain and suffering of others (whether they are in or out of their bodies), we open ourselves up to the possibility of experiencing their symptoms. Once again, we must keep in mind that the medium need not develop the actual disease or problem but merely temporarily experience the symptoms or characteristics.

GENERAL GUIDELINES
FOR A HEALING SEANCE

As always, decide on the purpose of the seance before you begin. If you are responding to a specific request for a healing seance from a member of your circle or a guest sitter, discuss ahead of time the nature of the person's ailment, depression, or problem. Up until now we have been focusing on physical ailments, but healing seances are equally effective with emotional problems such as anger, depression, and phobias (again, we must remember that healing circles are supplements to, not substitutes for, other professional treatments). Misfortune, bad luck, and disappointments such as result from loss of a job or family problems can also be addressed in seances.

Before the session begins, the medium should spend time talking with the client, both to get a sense of what the person's needs and expectations are and to prepare the client for what he or she can reasonably expect. Guest sitters should also be given more in-depth instructions so they can participate intelligently in the evening's work. The medium may also want to decide, in conjunction with the other sitters, what type of approach to take for the healing.

There are several ways to structure a healing seance. Use the needs of your client, the interest and skills of your sitters, and your own abilities as a medium to help you determine your agenda. Be creative and ready to improvise as you go if you feel it is right or the spirits instruct you to do so. A good guideline is to keep the client's needs foremost and, as always, detach yourself from your own needs, such as to impress others or to conduct the seance in your customary way because it feels more comfortable to you.

The Diagnostic Seance

If the client needs a diagnosis, proceed as you would in a regular seance where the purpose is to retrieve information. If your guide is capable of accessing this information and giving it to you, then that is what will happen. On the other hand, if your guide is not privy to this type of knowledge, he or she may have to summon another spirit, possibly a helping spirit associated with the client, to get the information.

Different guides work in different ways. If your guide gives you impressions or images rather than specific data, then relate those impressions and images to the client with as little interpretation as possible. For example, you might get an impression of the stomach or the lower back or some other area. Be content if that is all that comes through. It is always risky to jump to specific interpretations, such as "ulcer" for the stomach image or "slipped disk" for the lower back. Clients too should be content with whatever information is gathered, even though it may fall short of the precise details they had hoped for.

The same is true for treatment. A message may or may not include treatment. Or the treatment may be equally general, such as "change your diet," "see a physician," or "go into therapy." On the other hand, a spirit may give remarkably detailed and specific information. The famous psychic Edgar Cayce learned in trance the nature of illnesses and prescribed treatments even when they involved names and medical terms he had never heard of. But Cayce's abilities were truly spectacular; your guides may not be able to channel such specific information, so be content with what they can do. Remember, success depends on a personal and ongoing relationship with your spirit guides. Different spirits have different capabilities, and it is pointless to get angry or frustrated when they cannot deliver what you think they should.

Channeling Healing Energy

If a sitter requests healing energy, there are two approaches to choose from: circle-focused and sitter-focused.

When a sitter wishes to receive energy by simply being a member of the circle, the medium asks everyone to hold hands, close their eyes, and invoke the helping spirits. Then through either a group visualization or breathing meditation the medium leads the circle in raising energy.

There are various visualization techniques for raising energy. Here is a simple one. The medium asks the group to hold hands and requests that each sitter visualize the energy flowing into his or her body from both the earth and sky, coming up through the sitter's feet and down through the top of the head. The sitters are told to receive the energy from both directions into their heart areas and from there to allow it to flow throughout the body. When energy begins to build up within each individual, the medium asks the sitters to send the energy out through their left arms and hands into the hands of the people sitting to their left. At the same time, each sitter becomes aware of the energy entering his or her right hand. The medium instructs each sitter to feel the energy flow up his or her right arm, across the shoulders or chest, and down the left arm.

The leader may ask the sitters to visualize the energy in a certain way—as white light, a golden band, or a blue ribbon for instance—or to increase its velocity by visualizing it taking on greater speed. You can also expand it to a broad band of energy that eventually encloses everyone in the circle.

Allow the energy to revolve for a few moments. Then the medium asks each person to slow the movement down until it practically ceases and the circle is sitting in a strong field of gentle energy. Sit in silence for a few moments, enjoying the energy and the company of whatever personal spirits are attending.

This ritual obviously sends healing energy to everyone in the circle. The client who requested the healing participates on the same terms as everyone else. In many cases this is an effective healing experience. To focus more directly on the client, however, you can have each sitter silently send his or her energy, once it has built up sufficiently, directly toward the client, who is holding hands in the circle.

A variation on this client-focused procedure is to have the client sit in the center of the group (obviously this is not done around a table). The sitters hold hands and form a ring around the client. When the energy has been raised and calmed, and everyone sits in silence, each person directs energy toward the client in general or to specific areas of the body that need healing. Throughout the seance, the client, at the center of the circle, is like the hub of a wheel of energy. The sitters, like spokes on the wheel, send energy into the center from all directions.

Some people feel that energy, once raised, needs to be released in some formal manner. Others are content to let it dissipate naturally. If your group wants to release the energy, simply ask each person to allow the extra energy to flow back down through his or her legs and feet to return to the earth.

Laying On of Hands

Hands have been used for healing since the earliest recorded times, and certainly before that. Therapeutic Touch, as Dolores Krieger calls it, has had a long and respected history. Krieger points out how widespread the practice has been, citing, for example, the mysterious hand imprints painted on cave walls in the Pyrenees more than fifteen thousand years ago; ancient traditions of healing with the hands in India, Tibet, China, Egypt, and Chaldea; and Jewish and early Christian records that speak of the practice. Reference to healing with the hands can be found in the accounts of the Roman emperors Vespasian and Hadrian, legends associated with the Norwegian king Olaf, and in the medieval concept of the "king's touch," which was thought to cure certain ailments.

Although it is not necessary to hold a seance to lay on hands, the circle is a logical setting for it. The time spent communicating with the spirits and raising energy prepares both the sitters and the client for healing. You can develop your own methods, but here is a simple one. On chairs or on the floor, sitters form a circle around the client, who sits in the middle. The circle should be close enough so that everyone is within a few feet of the client. Sitters' hands do not have to physically touch the client's body once energy has been raised, although some clients may request this. If a client is not to be touched, sitters hold their hands a few inches from the client's body. (You should determine before the seance begins which method to use.)

If a client's ailment is localized in a specific part of

the body, you may direct all the energy to that place or have several sitters focus on that area while others send energy to other parts of the body. Do not become obsessed over whether you are sending energy into the exact spot. Energy is not time- and space-bound as are material objects. Energy is directed by our intention and attention as much as by our hands and will flow wherever we consciously put our attention.

Another variation is to try having the client lie on the floor in the center of the circle on a blanket and/or covered with a blanket. When it is time to direct energy through the hands, sitters hold their hands over or on different parts of the body. Depending on how many sitters are present, try to have someone at each foot or leg, each arm, the chest, stomach, hips, and of course the head. Another approach is to assign different chakra areas to sitters and direct energy toward these.

Removals

Energy is just energy; it is neutral. Nevertheless, human beings perceive it, as they do just about everything else, in moral terms. We think and speak of "good" and "bad" energy. Actually, if all the energy of the universe proceeds from the Divine Spirit, it must transcend our human categories of good and bad, as does the Divine Spirit Itself. For practical purposes, however, it is necessary to evaluate human situations in terms of some standards of good/bad, beneficial/harmful, safe/dangerous, and so forth. Illness, depression, misfortune, and other problems, therefore, appear to us as concentrations of negative energy or even the mischief caused by negative spirits.

For these reasons native healers and psychic healers in many cultures have ritual procedures for removing the harmful energy or spirits. Nature abhors a vacuum, and when we lose our own power or vital energy for whatever reason, other energy rushes in. In some places sickness is considered spirit intrusion; in other words, a spirit, force, or form of energy has entered the body and, although it may not be "evil" in itself, it is in the wrong place. (In some cultures it is believed that malicious people, especially hostile sorcerers, can cause harmful spirits or energies to enter a person.) The standard remedy for spirit intrusion is a form of extraction by which the healer pulls out or removes the unwanted energy.

In the context of a seance the medium, or all the sitters working together, can remove a client's unwanted energy. Usually what is removed is pain or a negative emotion, such as anger or fear, which has localized in a particular area of the body; it is replaced with energy that is healthy for the client. Here is how the unwanted energy can be removed.

Information about where the negative energy has collected is usually obtained during communication with the spirits previous to the healing. The spirits not only may indicate where in the body the emotion resides but also may suggest how the client should visualize it. Visualizing on the part of the client is an important aspect of the healing, for the client is not passive during the removal.

While the client is sitting or lying in the center of the circle, those sitters who are going to do the removal sit close and extend their right hands over the area of the body that is afflicted. The hands act as magnets, drawing pain, anger, or fear from the body. The client's role is to send the unwanted energies out of the body and into the waiting hands of the medium and sitters. The pain or emotion may be seen, for example, as a dark liquid stream flowing out of the body and into the hands. Or it may be visualized as a particular color.

In some cases the ailment may take the form of bugs, insects, rodents, or reptiles. Tribal shamans in some cultures "see" illness in the form of insects or reptiles, just as modern Western patients who visualize cancer cells and viruses often do. Mind-body studies related to illness indicate that it really doesn't matter what form the imagery takes so long as the patient associates the image with the illness and it is an image that the patient views as "conquerable." That is, the image of the illness is one that can be eradicated or "killed" in an appropriate visionary scenario. For example, the cancer cells or anger may be seen as green, scaly rodents, and the treatment (or medicine) takes the form of a wily cat that chases the rodents out of the system. A virus may be visualized as evil dwarfs, while the treatment is a heroic knight who battles the dwarfs to the death.

Often, rhythmic breathing can help clients expel unwanted energy. The client usually visualizes his or her breathing occurring at the place in the body that is afflicted. On the inhale the client visualizes his or her own energies collecting within the body. On the exhale the client pushes the harmful energy out of the body and into the healing hands of the sitters. The healers can also visualize the energy with the same imagery the client uses, or each person can see it in his or her own way.

Healers may feel sensations on the palm of the hand—tickling, prickling, temperature changes, increased pressure, itching—that indicate that they are receiving the unwanted energy. The reason that this harmful energy will not hurt the healers is twofold. First, the healers consciously receive the energy for the sake of the removal, and hence they have control over it. As we have said, energy of itself is neutral, and when we consciously take control over energy and use it for positive purposes, it causes no harm.

Second, there are ritual methods for releasing unwanted energy from the hands. The hand can be shaken
vigorously every few minutes or when the healing is completed. Another technique is to clap the hands once forcefully and blow across the palms immediately afterward.
Then, when the healing is over, sitters should rinse their
hands in clear water. Each of these methods releases the
energy back into the universe, where it exists as neutral
energy. It is not like turning something harmful loose into
the atmosphere, where it will go on to do more trouble.

To end the removal ritual, the medium asks the client
if he or she feels as if all the unwanted energy has been
removed or if it seems as if the group has removed all that
can be removed at the moment. If the client says no,
continue the removal. If the answer is yes, each person
discards the energy from his or her hands as just described.
To close the session, a few moments should be spent directing new energy into the person, filling the gaps left by the
removal.

Absent Healings

Many healing groups and seance circles perform healing
sessions for people not physically present, usually friends
and relatives of people in the circle. In some cases, where a
healer is well known, people in need may write or phone
requesting healings. The issue of absent healings raises
interesting ethical questions that each medium and circle
of sitters should consider carefully before doing this work.

The most ethical position we can take regarding healings is to do them only for someone who has given us
permission to do them. Never do a healing for someone
unless that person has explicitly asked for it. Sending
energy to heal or cure a person is intruding into another's
life, destiny, or karma. In whatever terms you put it, when

we heal, we meddle. It is presumptuous and (many believe) unethical to take action even for another person's "own good" because we cannot know for certain what is for another person's good, nor can we know for sure what another person would say is his or her "own good."

A classic example often cited is that of a person in a coma. Her family and friends pray that she recovers; healers send energy so that she regains consciousness while medical technology keeps her vital organs functioning. Everyone operates on the assumption that they know what is best for the woman, i.e., that she come out of the coma. In reality it may be that her time to pass on has come, and the coma is her means for doing that. A problem arises if we don't know the wishes of the woman.

Some ethicists might suggest that even the woman may not know what is best for her. Obviously this is true of everyone at any given moment. How can we ever be sure we know what is best for us? Perhaps we can't. And yet we have to live our lives as if we do know, taking reasonable steps to be as informed, sensitive, and truthful as possible so that we can make appropriate decisions. Most healers would say that if a person asks for healing energy to get well, save a marriage, land a certain job, or come out of a coma, there is nothing unethical in assuming the person knows what he or she wants. Healers then proceed to honor the person's wishes with whatever healing methods they use.

Is there anything we can do for someone we love or someone we know is having a hard time but who has not requested specific healing? Yes, there is. We can always ask our helping spirits to "send help." We can direct energy to another person with the explicit intention that either our helping spirits or the person's helping spirits use that energy in ways that are appropriate for the person's purpose in life. It may mean that the energy will be used to help the person pass on and make the transition into the next life. Or it may be used to help him or her recover from a serious illness. We leave it to the spirits to use the energy in the proper way. In doing so we attach no strings to our healing work. We do not send energy to "cure" illness or keep someone alive. We merely send help in the form of energy, intention, and our most heartfelt wishes. Furthermore, even if someone asks you specifically to help cure him, ease his personal sorrows, assuage some other pain, and you still feel that you might be intruding improperly in someone else's destiny, you can explicitly ask your own helping spirits (or the patient's) to render the energy ineffective if it is contrary to the individual's best interests on a more cosmic scale.

The procedure for absent healings is simple. When the seance has begun and the spirits are present, state or read the names, locations, and conditions of each person who has asked for a healing. The leader can read this information, or each sitter, speaking out loud, can add individuals that he or she knows about. Then proceed as you would to raise energy. When the energy has built up, the medium gives the signal to release it into the universe, where you trust the spirits to take it to the proper places.

Releasing energy can be done in several ways. You might, at the signal, raise your hands together, continuing to hold the hands of the persons on each side of you, and let the energy flow upward with that motion. Or you can break hands as you lift them, releasing the energy through your fingertips. Another method is to drop your neighbors' hands and cup your hands in front of you. Then let the energy in you collect in your hands in the form of a ball of light that grows large and bright. At a signal from the leader or medium, each person lifts his or her hands and blows forcefully on them, sending the ball of light up to the spirits.

Every person who comes for healing is unique. The more experienced you become, the better you will be able to evaluate and appreciate each person's unique qualities and circumstances and be able to give each person the healing experience he or she needs. Nevertheless, the key to successful healing seances is always the same: a humble willingness to serve as a channel between the suffering client and the spiritual sources of health and well-being, both in the greater universe and within each individual.

⚘ APPENDIX ⚘
How to Find a Medium

You may want to consult a medium for some personal reason, to study mediumship, or to invite him or her to sit with you in a development circle. Here are some guidelines for finding one and making sure he or she is trustworthy:

- Ask at your local metaphysical, spiritual, or occult bookstore if there are any mediums in your area. Sometimes mediums leave their business cards or fliers at bookstores.
- Call your community college or university and ask to speak to someone who teaches parapsychology. He or she may know of local mediums and psychics.
- Watch your local newspapers for advertisements of psychic fairs. You may be able to make some contacts through readers, healers, and other psychic practitioners.
- Call a local branch of the Spiritualist Church or a Unitarian-Universalist Church. Pastors or members of these churches can often put you in touch with

people who live alternative spiritual lifestyles and who may know mediums.

- The largest Spiritualist assembly in the United States is at Lily Dale, New York. Its address and phone number is
Lily Dale Spiritualist Community
5 Melrose Park
Lily Dale, NY 14752
(716) 595-8721 Fax: (716) 595-2442

Interview any mediums you find just as you would any professional. Find out how long they have been practicing, where they studied, or how they learned their skills. Ask what they charge. Ask for references from others who have used their services. And don't forget to listen to your instincts; if someone with impeccable references simply doesn't feel "right," continue your search.

ॐ ACKNOWLEDGMENTS ॐ

This book was inspired by the many people I know who are seeking, through various disciplines, to contact the spirit world. I am indebted to them for graciously taking time to share with me their knowledge, stories, and experience. I particularly wish to thank: Terri Thorley, Vickie Horton, Rose St. Hilaire, John Nakovich, Shyla O'Shea, Coleen Cannon, Diana McFarland Hein. I also thank my agent, Susan Lee Cohen, and my editor, Stacy Prince, for their invaluable assistance.